D1000362

THEOSOPHY ANSWERS SOME PROBLEMS OF LIFE

BY THE SAME AUTHOR

The Brotherhood of Angels and of Men
Be Ye Perfect
The Angelic Hosts
Fairies at Work and at Play
The Kingdom of Faerie
Health and the Spiritual Life
New Light on the Problem of Disease
An Occult View of Health and Disease
First Steps on the Path
Thus Have I Heard
The Inner Side of Church Worship
The Science of Seership
Clairvoyance and the Serpent Fire
The Coming of the Angels
Some Experiments in Four-Dimensional Vision
Destiny
The Miracle of Birth
Meditations on the Occult Life
Reincarnation: Fact or Fallacy?
The Seven Human Temperaments
The Kingdom of the Gods
Through the Gateway of Death
The Pathway to Perfection
A Yoga of Light
Occult Powers in Nature and in Man
Lecture Notes (The School of the Wisdom), Vols. I and II.
Man's Supersensory and Spiritual Powers
Authentic Stories of Intelligence in Animals
An Animals' Bill of Rights
Vital Questions Answered

THEOSOPHY ANSWERS SOME PROBLEMS OF LIFE

BY

GEOFFREY HODSON

THE THEOSOPHICAL PUBLISHING HOUSE
ADYAR, MADRAS 20, INDIA
1961

First Edition 1953
Second ,, 1955
Third ,, 1961

PRINTED IN INDIA

At the Vasanta Press, The Theosophical Society,
Adyar, Madras 20

INTRODUCTION

Mr. Hodson has produced a book which I believe will answer many questions that beset both the enquirer and the student. The splendid series of lectures delivered during his 1951 tour of Australia were condensed as radio talks and broadcast by Station 2GB Sydney, in the Sunday Theosophical Session. The scripts of these broadcasts have been collected and are now published in this most useful volume.

Every lecturer has his own particular presentation of Theosophy—ethical, sociological, psychological, philosophic or spiritual. He may combine many or all of these in a unity of presentation. Dr. Arundale used to call such expositions of the Ancient Wisdom as are collected in this volume " Straight Theosophy ", meaning fundamental Theosophy without any frills. Mr. Hodson calls them " Standard Theosophy ", which means much the same. Nevertheless Mr. Hodson, with his special gift of seership, gives due recognition to the psychic and the spiritual sides of life. This is all to the good, because he brings into clear focus both the inner worlds with their denizens and the spiritual realities upon which the outer world is founded. Furthermore, he has a gift, the fruit of long years of study and meditation, for the interpretation of the Christian Scriptures, and for correlating the Christian Faith with all the other great Faiths in a synthesis which might be characterised as a universal religion.

God speed this book. It will surely spread abroad the light of Truth and strengthen the hands of those engaged in the Great Work of teaching Theosophy and converting the world to Brotherhood.

J. L. DAVIDGE,
General Secretary,
The Theosophical Society,
Australian Section.

THEOSOPHY AND THE THEOSOPHICAL SOCIETY

THE word *Theosophia*, derived from two Greek words meaning Divine Wisdom, was coined by the Neo-Platonists in the Second Century of the Christian era to connote the truths revealed to man by his Evolutionary Elders at the dawn of human life on this planet, and added to, checked and rechecked down to the present day by an unbroken succession of Adept[1] occult investigators. The full fruits of this dual process have been preserved by the still-living Hierophants and Initiates of

[1] *Adept.* An Initiate of the 5th degree; a Master in the Science of Esoteric Philosophy; a perfected man; an exalted Being who has attained mastery over the human nature and possesses knowledge and power commensurate with lofty evolutionary stature. This fulfilment of human destiny is thus described by St. Paul: "Till we all come in the unity of the faith, and of the knowledge of the Son of God, unto a perfect man, unto the measure of the stature of the fulness of Christ." (*Eph.* IV. 13.) Certain Adepts remain on earth to assist humanity and are referred to by St. Paul as "just men made perfect". (*Heb.* XII. 23.) The Lord Christ similarly described the destiny of man in His words: "Ye therefore shall be perfect, as your heavenly Father is perfect." (*Matt.* V. 48. R. V.)

the Greater Mysteries, in which they were imparted to pledged neophytes alone. In their doctrinal aspect, these Mysteries consist of a vast body of teaching which embraces every conceivable subject to which the mind of man can be turned.

The fundamental principles of religion, philosophy, art, science and politics are all contained within this Wisdom of the Ages. From the time of the closing of the Neo-Platonic and Gnostic Schools to the last quarter of the Nineteenth Century, save for the few alchemists, Kabbalists, Rosicrucians, occultly instructed Masons and Christian mystics, Theosophy was unknown in the Western world. Before then it was known and studied in various forms by the Platonists, the Pythagoreans, the Egyptians, and the Chaldeans, whilst in India and China it has been preserved down the ages in unbroken continuity. It is the wisdom of the *Upanishads* and the *Vedas*, the very heart of Hinduism, Taoism and Islam. By means of allegory and symbol it is revealed in the Christian Scriptures, the dead-letter reading of which has blinded Christians to their deeper significance.

The Theosophical Society, founded in New York in 1875, a reincarnation of innumerable similar Movements in the past, is one of the many channels chosen from time to time by the Teachers of the Race for the transmission of this Ancient Wisdom to man. Theosophists are offered the opportunity of studying, living and presenting the age-old truths to the world in terms of modern thought. Though the presentations may vary, Theosophy itself, being all-Truth, is unchanging and external.

The study of comparative religion reveals the existence of certain doctrines which are common to all World Faiths. Although differently presented in each, when collected and blended into a whole these teachings constitute a basic body of revealed Truth which can be studied independently of all religious systems Each world religion reveals an arc of the circle of Eternal Wisdom. Theosophy, although as yet but partially revealed to man, is the full circle of Truth. Age by age, at the direction of Those who are the Guardians of knowledge and its accompanying power, aspects of the Eternal Wisdom are revealed to man through world religions and philosophies.

The great practical value of Theosophy consists in its revelation of the meaning and purpose of human existence, which without it is a hopeless puzzle defying solution. A puzzle may be solved by two methods. One is that of trial and error, of experimenting with various pieces in the hope that ultimately they will fit together. This is a slow and unsatisfactory method, particularly in the attempt to solve the problems of life. The other method, far more satisfactory, is based on pre-knowledge of the position of the various pieces in the complete design. Theosophy provides that knowledge, reveals the due place in an evolutionary plan of every individual and every event.

Life somewhat resembles a piece of tapestry. On the underside one sees little save incomprehensible tangles, knots, badly blended colours and a general confusion. Examination of the upper side, however, reveals the whole pattern, shows that the confusion is only apparent, since every juxtaposition is essential to the completion of the design. So, also, the apparent confusion in the lives of individuals and of Nations. Theosophy reveals the plan of life, thereby bestowing mental serenity upon those who study it and making intelligent and purposeful living possible for them.

The student of Theosophy will do well to recognise that the human mind, being finite, cannot fully comprehend abstract Truth, which is infinite. As the human intellect develops, man's power of comprehension increases. Truth appears to change, as does the shape of a mountain gradually approached and seen from different points of view. The mountain itself is, however, relatively changeless, as also is eternal Truth. Theosophy being all-Truth, no final theosophical statement is ever possible. No theosophical teacher can legitimately make authoritative pronouncements. In the Theosophical Society opinion is therefore free, save, perhaps, concerning the brotherhood of man, which tends to be regarded as a fact in Nature to be recognised rather than as a dogma to be enforced. With this exception no theosophical utterance is binding upon another and no statement is regarded as representing final Truth.

The Theosophical Society is officially described as being "composed of students, belonging to any religion in the world or to none, who are united by their approval of the society's objects, by their wish to remove religious antagonisms and to draw together men of goodwill, whatsoever their religious opinions, and by their desire to study religious truths and to share the results of their studies with others. Their bond of union is not the profession of a common belief, but a common search and aspiration for Truth. They hold that Truth should be sought by study, by reflection, by purity of life, by devotion to high ideals, and they regard Truth as a prize to be striven for, not as a dogma to be imposed by authority. They consider that belief should be the result of individual study or intuition, and not its antecedent, and should rest on knowledge, not on assertion. They extend tolerance to all, even to the intolerant, not as a privilege they bestow but as a duty they perform, and they seek to remove ignorance, not to punish it. They see every religion as an expression of the Divine Wisdom and prefer its study to its condemnation, and its practice to proselytism. Peace is their watchword, as Truth is their aim.

"Theosophy is the body of truths which forms the basis of all religions, and which cannot be claimed as the exclusive possession of any. It offers a philosophy which renders life intelligible, and which demonstrates the justice and the love which guide its evolution. It puts death in its rightful place, as a recurring incident in an endless life, opening the gateway to a fuller and more radiant existence. It restores to the world the Science of the Spirit, teaching man to know the Spirit as himself and the mind and body as his servants. It illuminates the Scriptures and doctrines of religions by unveiling their hidden meanings, and thus justifying them at the bar of intelligence, as they are ever justified in the eyes of intuition."

On December 23rd, 1924, the General Council of the Theosophical Society passed the following Resolution affirming freedom of thought within the Society:

"As the Theosophical Society has spread far and wide over the civilized world, and as members of all religions have become members of it without surrendering the special dogmas, teachings and beliefs of their respective faiths, it is thought desirable to emphasize the fact that there is no doctrine, no opinion, by whomsoever taught or held, that is in any way binding on any member of the Society, none which any member is not free to accept or reject. Approval of its three Objects is the sole condition of membership. No teacher or writer, from H. P. Blavatsky downwards, has any authority to impose his teachings or opinions on members. Every member has an equal right to attach himself to any teacher or to any school of thought which he may choose, but has no right to force his choice on any other. Neither a candidate for any office, nor any voter, can be rendered ineligible to stand or to vote, because of any opinion he may hold, or because of membership in any school of thought to which he may belong. Opinions or beliefs neither bestow privileges nor inflict penalties. The Members of the General Council earnestly request every member of the Theosophical Society to maintain, defend and act upon these fundamental principles of the Society, and also fearlessly to exercise his own right of liberty of thought and of expression thereof, within the limits of courtesy and consideration for others."

Despite this complete absence of dogmatism, which should be the hallmark of all expositions of Theosophy, there does exist a general body of teaching, a synthesis of the common doctrines of world philosophies and religions, ancient and modern, which in practice is generally accepted *as long as it rings true*. Apart from the development and use of supersensory powers as a means of research, this constitutes a test which each student can apply to all theosophical teachings: *do they ring true*? If an affirmative answer is possible, they may be accepted as working hypotheses until fuller knowledge proves or disproves them. Should a statement not ring true, three courses are open to the student. He may reject, ignore, or suspend judgment until by self-training he develops the capacity to discover the facts for himself. The last of these three courses would appear to be the most desirable. Thus the attitude of mind in which Theosophy should be studied is that of the scientist—the acceptance of a well-supported theory as a working hypothesis until it is proved, disproved or suspended.

The writings of Madame H. P. Blavatsky constitute the primary source of Theosophical information in modern literature. Though branded as a charlatan by those who have neither investigated her life nor understood her literary work, this great lady is revered by tens of thousands of students of Theosophy as a light-bringer to the modern world. They believe her to have been chosen for this mission by the Sages [1] who have been both Guardians and Revealers of Theosophy to man throughout the ages. These Adepts used Madame

[1] *Vide The Masters*, by A. Besant.

Blavatsky as an amanuensis and with her aid gave Theosophy to the world in our time. Two main methods were employed. One consisted of fully conscious clairvoyance and mental telepathy in which, as a result of training under Them, she was highly skilled. The other method was that of the occult precipitation of letters written by Them, or by Their disciples at Their direction.

By the first method Madame Blavatsky produced her two great works, *Isis Unveiled* and *The Secret Doctrine*—each an almost inexhaustible fount of esoteric wisdom and knowledge. By the second method Mr. A. P. Sinnett, at that time (1880) editor of India's leading newspaper, *The Pioneer*, obtained the material for his books, *The Occult World*, *Esoteric Buddhism* and *The Growth of the Soul*. These authors have been followed by many others, notably Dr. Annie Besant and Bishop C. W. Leadbeater, both of whom, in addition to the receipt of direct instruction from the Sages, were trained by Them in the development of occult powers and their use as a means of research. Their subsequent contribution to human knowledge is immense.

The late Dr. G. S. Arundale and Mr. C. Jinarājadāsa, past Presidents, and Mr. N. Sṛi Ram, the fifth and present President of the Theosophical Society, all of whom are greatly respected theosophical leaders, teachers and authors, have also made their own valuable contributions. Mr. Jinarājadāsa has collected and published many of the letters of the Sages to Mr. Sinnett and others, in three volumes entitled *Letters of the Masters of the Wisdom*, Series I and II, and *The K. H. Letters to C. W. Leadbeater*. The interested reader is referred to these various sources as the bases for most of the statements made in this book. Since they are admittedly both general and incomplete, each of my main sentences should be prefaced by some such phrase as " According to my limited understanding ". As this would be tedious, I ask that it be regarded as implicit throughout this theosophical study of the problems of life.

GEOFFREY HODSON

PREFACE

In this volume of published Australian broadcasts, the conversational, broadcast style has been largely retained. Additional material has been included, quotations have been checked and their references given and some further, apposite sayings from world literature have been added. A number of the opening paragraphs, in which problems are enunciated, were not part of the original broadcasts. Three broadcasts on the life after death are not included, as they form part of a new book entitled *Through the Gateway of Death.*

The terms " Theosophy answers ", " Theosophy teaches " and " Theosophy says " are technically impermissible, because Theosophy is the Eternal Wisdom. It cannot therefore be said to " speak ". An exponent of Theosophy personally interprets its teachings and applies them to the problems of life, as I have done in these Talks, and it is in this sense that I have used the terms referred to. The sun neither rises nor sets, but the astronomically incorrect words " sunrise " and " sunset " have come into common use to save such long sentences as " the revolution of the earth round its axis once in every twenty-four hours produces the illusion of sunrise and sunset." A similar verbal economy supports the use of the above phrases concerning Theosophy.

Since fundamental theosophical teachings formed the bases of all these weekly broadcasts, and were repeated in many of them, a certain repetitiveness, particularly of those teachings, appears in this work. Since readers may on occasion refer merely to one or more subjects and at any given time read those broadcasts only, the repetitions are retained.

GEOFFREY HODSON

Epsom,
Auckland, N.Z.
1953

CONTENTS

PART FIVE

WORLD PEACE AND OUR PERSONAL RESPONSIBILITY

PART SIX

THE LAWS OF HEALTH AND HAPPINESS

CHAPTER PAGE

PART SEVEN

ANIMAL WELFARE: MAN'S GREAT RESPONSIBILITY

PART ONE

MAN, HIS NATURE AND HIS DESTINY

CHAPTER I

FROM MAN TO SUPERMAN

"What is man, that thou art mindful of Him?" [1]

THE English poet, Alexander Pope (1688-1744), referred to this fundamental problem concerning the nature of man when he said: "The proper study of mankind is man". The teachings of Theosophy enable one to follow this advice with great fullness and completeness; for Theosophy teaches not only of the physical, material man, but also of his intellectual and spiritual nature and powers.

I am going to put before you, as concisely as possible, some of the age-old teachings about man which form part of what is known as the Ancient Wisdom or Theosophy. What, then, is he? How is he described? The Theosophical definition of man makes him primarily a threefold individual, for he is described as that being in whom highest spirit and lowest matter are united by intellect.

Although threefold in essence, man is also said to be manifest in seven ways, or to express himself at seven levels of consciousness and degrees of density of matter

[1] *Ps.* VIII. 4.

through seven appropriate vehicles. Of these seven bodies of man the physical is the most dense, the other six being built of finer and finer gradations of substance until the highest, most tenuous and most spiritual body is reached. Thus he is a threefold, immortal, spiritual being, incarnated in four mortal, material bodies.

Man, Mortal and Immortal

The three parts of man's spiritual nature are reflections in him of the Will, the Wisdom and the Intelligence of the Supreme Deity, the Blessed Trinity. The pertinent teaching concerning both the Deity and man is that they are threefold; for God, the Trinity, reproduces Himself as the threefold Spiritual Soul of man, or as the Bible puts it, man is made in God's image.[1] In this spiritual aspect of his nature, man, sometimes called the microcosm (little world), is for ever one with the Divine or Macrocosm (great world). The " immortal and eternal God Who for ever reigneth serene above the waterfloods " and the Spirit of man are one Spirit. Thus the Deity is in no sense either external to man or, in essence, different from him. They are one and indivisible throughout all eternity. This is the great truth concerning man and in it resides the secret of supreme achievement, the attainment of Godlike power and undisturbable peace.

When the individual fully realises his unity with God, the power of the Cosmos is then at his disposal.

[1] *Gen.* I. 26.

The distinction between the Logos of a Universe and the Deity in man lies neither in location nor in essential nature, but only in the degree in which the triune powers are expressed. In God these are perfected, but in man they become manifest in a gradually increasing degree of fullness as his evolution proceeds. Ultimately they will be fully unfolded in him, as they now are in the Deity. This, the Ancient Wisdom teaches, is the destiny of man—fully to make manifest inherent deific powers.

This brings us to the next thought, which is that in the divine aspect of his nature man is immune from death. The Theosophical solution of the problem of death is that the essential, inner man is immortal. Only the outer personality passes away. Individuality, capacities, character, interests and affections, however, all persist after bodily death. Furthermore, all the faculties attained during life are permanent powers of the threefold Inner Self of man.

Mind, Emotion, Vitality, and Flesh

Now we must consider man's four material bodies. In the order of their density, beginning at the most refined, these are: his mental body, composed of mental material or "mind stuff", his vehicle of thought; his emotional body, composed of somewhat denser material, his vehicle of feeling; his vital or etheric body, composed of ether, the subtle fluid permeating space, the conserving principle of his physical vital forces and the link between the superphysical and physical vehicles;

the physical body, composed of solid, liquid and gaseous material, the vehicle of action and self-expression in the physical world. These four denser bodies are subject to death and disintegration.

The Body, a Temple of an Indwelling God

When man is conscious solely in this fourfold material and mortal aspect of his nature, he is temporarily unconscious both of his divinity and of his unity with God; as his evolution proceeds, however, he gradually rediscovers this lost knowledge of oneness with the Deity. This is the immediate object of all spiritual endeavours. Especially is it the goal of all who seek the way of illumination. To know by continuing direct experience that God and man are identical beings is to have discovered the ultimate secret of life, the *summum bonum* of human knowledge.

An ancient ritual says: " As God is the centre of His Universe, so is His reproduction of Himself the centre of man's existence, the Inner Ruler Immortal."

Angela Morgan wrote a beautiful poem entitled " Passports ", expressing the same truth. One verse reads:

> " Hurl thou thy cry at Heaven's gate—
> God must admit thee soon or late.
> Thy passport? Saints could ask no more,
> His image at thy very core."

The salvation of man, following his so-called " Fall " (descent of his Spiritual Self into matter), is an ascent into full experience of this transcendent fact—God's image at his very core.

The Sublime Purpose of Human Life

Why, then, we may now ask, is the human Spirit incarnate in a physical body? The purpose of man's existence is evolution and this is a dual process, being partly spiritual and partly bodily. Evolution consists on the one hand of the gradual unfoldment from latency to full potency of man's threefold spiritual attributes, and on the other hand of the development of his four material vehicles to a condition in which these powers are perfectly expressed. The two processes are parallel. Inner unfoldment is accompanied by outer development, the unified and harmonised mortal bodies together becoming an ever more worthy temple of the Inner God.

This is the solution of the problem of the purpose of life, which is glorious in the extreme, the goal of human evolution being the standard of perfection described by St. Paul as the "perfect man, . . . the measure of the stature of the fullness of Christ." [1] This implies the attainment of a divine state of omnipotence or perfected [2] and resistless will, omnipresence or perfected and all-embracing love, and omniscience or perfected and all-inclusive knowledge. Furthermore, and most important, the attainment of this perfection is absolutely certain for the Spiritual Self of every

[1] *Eph.* IV. 13.

[2] Theosophically, perfection is reached only in a relative sense, man's future power, wisdom and splendour being entirely without limit.

human being. The command: " Be ye therefore perfect, even as your Father which is in heaven is perfect ",[1] will one day be literally obeyed by every man. All God's sons will one day reach His feet, however far they stray.

The Existence of Perfected Men

We now come to another most important Theosophical idea. This goal of human perfection has already been reached by certain men and women. Such Personages are known as World Saviours, Rishis, Mahatmas, Adepts and Masters[2] of the Wisdom. Together, these Elder Brethren of humanity constitute the Inner Government of our world. They are the true spiritual Teachers and Inspirers of men, the august body of " just men made perfect "[3] referred to by St. Paul, the Communion of Saints, the Great White Brotherhood of Adepts.

How is this state of human perfection or Adeptship attained? By a succession of lives here on earth. The goal of Adeptship is reached by means of repeated incarnations in the four material vehicles of the mortal man. This important subject of rebirth is considered in Part Two of this volume.

The Doctrine of Rebirth

Man's successive lives are connected with each other by the operation of the universal law of cause and effect, compensation or readjustment. All actions, feelings

[1] *Matt.* V. 48.

[2] Technically applied to Adepts who take pupils.

[3] *Heb.* XII. 23.

and thoughts produce their own natural and perfectly appropriate reactions. These may follow their cause immediately, later in the same life, or in succeeding incarnations. Under this compensatory law actions motived by love, service, unselfishness and kindness produce a pleasure and a growing freedom of self-expression which encourage the actor to repeat them. Actions motived by dislike, greed, selfishness and cruelty produce a pain and an increasing limitation of self-expression which discourage the actor from repeating them. Such is the law. Suffering is not a retribution imposed by the Deity, a punishment inflicted from above, nor is it an accidental adversity. All pain is self-inflicted and, moreover, is designed to inform the actor of his transgressions. The law is therefore truly beneficent and educative in its ultimate purpose and effect.

The Way of Sorrow's Ceasing

The way of escape from sorrow is defined in the Sermon on the Mount and in that teaching of the Lord Buddha which is known as "The Noble Eightfold Path". Here are the eight ways of life infallibly leading to enduring happiness: Right Belief, Right Thought, Right Speech, Right Action, Right Means of Livelihood, Right Exertion or Energy, Right Remembrance and Right Meditation. The Lord Buddha summed up these teachings in the following words: to cease from sin, to get virtue, to purify the heart, to serve the world.

Such are some of the teachings of Theosophy concerning man.

CHAPTER II

THE SEVENFOLD KEY TO HUMAN CHARACTER

The Complexity of Human Nature

As one's knowledge of humanity grows, one is continually confronted with the problems of understanding one's fellow men and of working harmoniously with those possessing qualities of character markedly different from one's own. One cannot but be impressed by the almost infinite variety of human beings, by the richness of individuality amongst mankind and by the great diversity of human gifts. Humanity includes the dauntless explorer and the gentle nun; the soldier and the hermit, the monk or the recluse; the politician; the businessman and woman outwardly active in world affairs; the scientist and the scholar immersed in their researches. All these and many other opposite and diverse types go to the making of mankind.

Seven Types of Human Beings

Is there a key by means of which human nature may be understood and this complexity of human types may be comprehended and reduced to order?

Theosophy answers " yes ", and further says that the key is numerical, the governing number being seven. Thus there are seven main types of human beings, each with its outstanding natural attributes and qualities. All powers are within every human being, but in each there is a preponderant tendency and power. Discovering this, a key is found to the understanding of human nature.

What are these seven outstanding qualities and what are the types of men by whom they are exemplified? The subject is immense and I can but refer those who are interested to Theosophical literature on the subject of the " Seven Rays ", as they are called. The reason for this name—" Rays "—is that man's innate powers are due to the presence of a particular Ray of the Divine Light shining predominantly in a man or a woman. All the seven Rays—I will use that term from now on—are in everyone, and all must eventually be developed to the highest possible degree; but throughout the evolutionary process the basic Ray quality will predominate.

The Ray of Power

The first of these Rays is that of power, a Ray from the First Aspect of the Blessed Trinity, the Almighty Creator and Father of the Universe and of all that it contains. Such men are characterised by the qualities of power, will, courage, leadership and self-reliance. They are the great soldiers, the explorers, the rulers and the statesmen. Aggressive dictators who become tyrants are examples of the misdirection for destructive purposes of the Will of God as it becomes active in them. Ultimately this tremendous power will be turned to constructive purposes only, to the attainment of victory over the lower nature, and to the conquest and exploration of the higher aspects of the Divine in man and in Nature. These people become great spiritual leaders, and, indeed, spiritual kings. The explorer's ideal, " To strive, to seek, to find and not to yield ", is typical of the first Ray.

The Ray of Universal Love

The second Ray is that of wisdom and universal love, of spiritual insight and intuition. These qualities are generally combined with a deep sense of that oneness with others from which compassion and sympathy are born. The type of man is the sage, the natural-born teacher and healer of the world, the reformer and the lover of his fellow men. This love often overflows to include the members of the lower kingdoms of Nature. The great humanitarians and all lovers and protectors of the members of the animal kingdom, like St. Francis, thus display the qualities of the second of the Seven Rays. In them the Second or Christ Aspect of the Blessed Trinity is predominant, and their destiny is to become Christlike in all-embracing love and wisdom. The phrase " Love is not love which alters when it alteration finds " partly expresses the second Ray ideal of love.

Philosopher and Strategist

The third Ray is that of creative ideation, intellectual comprehension, and understanding of life and of the principles and laws of life. The qualities of adaptability, impartiality and tact are predominant in third Ray people, who often possess a penetrative and interpretative mind. The type of man is the philosopher, but also the ambassador, the diplomat, the strategist, the organiser, the chess-player and the judge. The great Generals of today need to possess both the indomitable and combative will power of the first Ray and the organising and strategic ability of the third. Field-Marshal Montgomery is a good example of this blending, for he is described as a swift and fluid tactician, ready when necessary to revise the whole scheme of an attack, as he successfully did in the desert at Mareth when a stiff Nazi counter-attack upset the plan of battle. The Psalmist's words, " Give me understanding, and I shall keep Thy law ",[1] express the point of view of this Ray.

Artist

The fourth Ray, midway as it is between the first and the second triplicity of the seven, is the Ray of harmony, of balance, of beauty and of rhythm. The type of man, therefore, is the artist, though the artistic expression and medium chosen will be influenced by the presence and activity of other Rays. These people make the best artists, actors and, in some ways, the

[1] *Ps.* CXIX. 34.

best teachers. They dramatise their subjects, illustrate them and elevate people by the power of beauty. The words of Keats exemplify the artist's highest ideal: "We must worship the principle of beauty in all things", and "'Beauty is truth, truth beauty,'—that is all ye know on earth, and all ye need to know." [1]

Scientist

The fifth Ray is that of mental analysis and other attributes of the formal mind of man, that which is generally called the legal mentality, capable of reasoning correctly from effect to cause and of deducing a central, general truth from a number of particulars. Such are the great mathematicians, scientists, lawyers and detectives. Scott, the great explorer, who was a many-sided man, with leadership (first Ray) as an outstanding attribute, displayed a fifth Ray outlook when he said: "Science is the rock foundation of all effort". Scott has been described as "an undefeatable sportsman, buoyant, indomitable", these also being first Ray qualities.

Crusader and Martyr

The sixth Ray is that of fiery enthusiasm, ardour, one-pointedness, devotion and sacrificial love. Sixth Ray people are the mystics, the devotees, the evangelists, and often the martyrs, who count life well lost in the service and furtherance of a great Cause. General William Booth, the great founder of the Salvation

[1] *Ode on a Grecian Urn*, Keats.

Army, was, in that work, a blend of the sixth and first Rays, for in serving his Master and his fellow men he employed the military method of the first Ray. To regard loyalty as " the marrow of honour " and to be " faithful unto death " are ideals of those following the sixth Ray.

Ordered Activity

The seventh Ray is that of power in action, of ordered activity, of grace and precision. Nobility, chivalry, the military method and a general magnificence, are also shown by seventh Ray people. The type of man is the ceremonialist, the ritualist, the pageant master, the producer, and the man and woman of true knightliness and royalty. Love of magic, of splendour and of perfection—" If a thing is worth doing, it is worth doing well "—are attributes of those on the seventh Ray.

Predominant Ideals

Such, very briefly described, are some of the qualities of the seven Rays. As I have said, all the Rays are in each one of us, though the method and characteristic of one Ray will generally predominate. In the main the ideal adopted by Scott, and taken from Tennyson's " Ulysses ", truly characterises the first Ray: " To strive, to seek, to find and not to yield." Wilson's advice to Oates in the Antarctic, when his feet were becoming useless, was " Slog on, just slog on." There, in excelsis, you have one of the great qualities of the first Ray.

For people of the second Ray there is no religion higher than love, no achievement greater than effective and loving service. They would agree with the poet who said: " Those who walk in love may wander far, but God will bring them where the blessed are."

The third Ray is well exemplified in the Cavendish family motto: " Cavendo tutus ", meaning " Secure by caution ". Their prayer would be: " Give me understanding, and I shall keep Thy law; yea, I shall observe it with my whole heart." [1] The motto of the Theosophical Society, also that of the Maharajah of Benares, is third Ray in quality: " There is no religion higher than truth."

The highest spiritual ideal of the fourth Ray is exemplified in a saying of H. P. Blavatsky, the great Co-Founder of the Theosophical Society in 1875. Madame Blavatsky said: " What the true occultist seeks is not knowledge or growth or happiness or power for himself; but having become conscious that the harmony of which he forms part is broken on the outer plane he seeks the means to dissolve that discord into a higher harmony."

The driving force of the fifth Ray is well defined by Anton J. Carlson, who said: " The greatest thing in science is the scientific method, rechecked observation and experiments, objectively recorded with absolute honesty and without fear or favour. Science in this sense has as yet scarcely touched the common man or his leaders."

[1] *Ps.* CXIX. 34.

The attribute of the sixth Ray is wonderfully expressed in a speech by Mr. Churchill to all Ministers of his Cabinet other than War Cabinet Ministers, repeated in the Second Volume of his Memoirs, called " Their Finest Hour ". The time is just before Dunkirk and Churchill writes: " We were perhaps twenty-five round the table. I described the course of events and I showed them plainly where we were and all that was in the balance. Then I said quite casually, and not treating it as a point of special significance, ' Of course, whatever happens at Dunkirk we shall fight on! ' Then there occurred a demonstration which . . . surprised (me) . . . there was a white glow, overpowering, sublime, which ran through them, and through our island from end to end." That white glow is typical of the burning ardour and fiery fervour of the sixth Ray.

Co-ordination and the synthesising of the many into the one are outstanding characteristics of those on the seventh Ray. The ideals are physical efficiency, perfection, order in all the conduct of life, power perfectly and irresistibly made manifest.

Many Pathways to Perfection

Part of the great value of this knowledge of the seven Rays is that it breeds tolerance born of understanding —particularly towards those from whom one differs. Each human being is seen to be following his own road to his own goal. When not harmful to others that way must be respected, even though it may be very different from one's own. This is beautifully expressed in a Hindu Scripture in which the Lord of the Universe, speaking through the lips of Shri Krishna, says in effect: "However men approach Me, even so do I welcome them, for the path men take from every side is Mine." [1]

[1] *Bhagavad Gita*, IV. 11, translated by A. Besant.

CHAPTER III

THE HUMAN AURA, ITS COLOURS AND THEIR MEANINGS

The Deeps of Human Nature

THERE is an old saying that still waters run deep, and it is common experience that time is required in order to understand and appreciate the deeper and finer qualities of one's fellow men. Yet these are present when first we meet people, though unperceived. Each person has characteristics which only long association enables one to discover. In what form, then, do the qualities of human nature exist? Do we all carry our characters about with us and, if so, where and in what form? Furthermore, are there any means by which our capacities, our habits and tendencies and our outlook on life can be quickly perceived?

The Invisible Worlds

World religions and philosophies answer these problems. They teach that the visible Universe is the outer physical manifestation of an inner, hidden Life; that this inner aspect is the reality and the outer, temporal world its reflection or shadow. Much information is available concerning the invisible Universe. It is said to occupy the same space as the material planets, to interpenetrate and vivify them and also to extend far beyond them out into space. The inner world is one of light, its substance self-radiant, glowing with myriad hues. It is inhabited by its own teeming population and has its own scenery and conditions.

This world of light and life and innumerable presences is here and now and all about us, but normally it is invisible. This is because its forces vibrate on higher frequencies than our senses can respond to. At death man transfers and limits his life to this inner world, partakes of its life and becomes subservient to its laws. Nevertheless, even while in the earthly body man also has his existence in these superphysical realms, for he possesses and uses vehicles of consciousness made of their substances. Thus Theosophy teaches that man is very much more than this physical body and nature. Maeterlinck said: " Every existing body is prolonged in time and space. Its head is bathed in duration and its feet are rooted in extension."

The Invisible Self of Man

Normally we see nothing whole, but only cross-sections of totality. This is especially true when we first meet other people. Time reveals more of individuals. We say that people " grow on us ". Nevertheless, all that we later discover was there from the first, but unperceived. The whole man is present at every moment of waking life, but fuller comprehension of people's natures and characters dawns slowly upon us. Both the past and the future of every human being also may be said to be present, if only in terms of both germinal potentialities and developed powers and faculties. Fully perceived, the complete man, physical, emotional, mental and spiritual, would be revealed, as also would his whole character and capacity—past, present and to come. Even the humblest man or woman would then be found to possess very great potential qualities and powers.

The Colours of the Aura

In what form do these unseen attributes exist and how do they appear? Theosophy answers, "They exist and may be seen as light." Superphysically, every man is robed in a luminous vesture. The human Soul is veritably a being of light, and each power and quality shines out in its own hue. Every man is thus a Joseph, clothed with a coat of many colours,[1] each representing a power, a quality, a faculty, or a characteristic. The interpretation of the colours of the aura in terms of human qualities is in itself a science. All of the superphysical bodies of man are brilliantly coloured and the significance of each hue varies somewhat according to the vehicle in which it appears. In offering some Theosophical ideas upon the subject, I here confine myself to the emotional nature of man and his astral [2] aura.

[1] *Gen.* XXXVII. 3.

[2] *Astral.* The name given by medieval theosophists to the emotional body, doubtless on account of its self-luminous appearance.

The astral vehicle not only permeates the physical body but also surrounds it in every direction like a cloud. That portion which extends beyond the limits of the physical body is usually termed the astral " aura ". The aura is ovoid in shape and about three times the size of the physical body. The central portion of the astral body takes the exact form of the physical and is, in fact, quite clearly distinguishable from the surrounding aura. It is usually termed the astral counterpart. The exact correspondence of the astral body with the physical is, however, merely a matter of external form and does not involve any similarity of function in the various organs.

To clairvoyant sight one of the principal features of an astral body consists of its colours, which constantly play through it and express in astral matter human feelings, passions, emotions, desires. All known shades—and many which are at present unknown to us—exist upon each of the superphysical planes of Nature. At every ascending level they become more delicate and more luminous, so that they might be described as higher octaves of colour. Here is a list of the principal hues in the astral aura and the emotions of which they are an expression.

The Meaning of the Colours

Black: Hatred and malice; deep red flashes on a black ground indicate rage.

A Scarlet Cloud: Irritability.

Brilliant Scarlet: Noble indignation.

Lurid and sanguinary Red: Sensuality.

Dull, hard Brown-grey: Selfishness.

Dull, almost Rust-red: Avarice. This colour is usually arranged in parallel bars across the astral body, illustrating the act that the miser is self-imprisoned.

Greenish-brown, lit up by deep red or scarlet flashes: Jealousy.

Heavy, leaden Grey: Depression. Like the brown red of avarice, grey is often arranged in parallel lines, conveying the impression of a cage.

Livid Grey: Fear, which can spread to cause panic.

Dull and heavy Crimson: Selfish love.

Rose: Unselfish love. When exceptionally brilliant and tinged with lilac, spiritual love for humanity.

Orange: Pride or ambition.

Yellow: Intellect. This colour varies from a deep and dull tint, through brilliant gold, to clear and luminous lemon or primrose yellow, according to the use to which the intellect is put.

Dull Yellow Ochre: Mental faculty applied to selfish purposes.

Clear Gamboge: Unselfish mental activity.

Primrose Yellow: Intellect devoted to spiritual ends.

Gold: Pure intellect applied to philosophy or mathematics.

Green: In general, adaptability.

Grey green: Deceit and cunning.

Emerald Green: Versatility, ingenuity and resourcefulness unselfishly applied.

Pale, Luminous Blue-green: Deep sympathy and compassion. The power of perfect adaptability.

Bright Apple-green: Strong vitality.

Dark clear Blue: Religious feeling. It is liable to be tinged by many other qualities, thus varying from indigo, through a deep violet to muddy grey-blue, according to the quality of the devotion.

Light Blue: Devotion to a noble spiritual ideal.

Luminous Lilac-blue (usually accompanied by sparkling golden stars): The higher spirituality with lofty spiritual aspirations.

Joy shows itself in a general brightening and radiance of both the mental and the astral bodies, and in a peculiar rippling of the surface of the aura. Cheerfulness manifests as a modified bubbling form of this rippling effect. Surprise is shown in the aura by a sharp constriction of the mental body, usually communicated to both the astral and the physical bodies.

Reading the Aura

As human emotions are hardly ever unmixed, so these colours are seldom perfectly pure. More usually they are mixtures. The purity of many colours can be dimmed by the hard brown-grey of selfishness, or tinged with the deep orange of pride. In reading the full meaning of colours other points have also to be taken into consideration, such as the general brilliance of the astral body, the comparative definiteness or indefiniteness of its outline and the relative brightness of the different centres of force.

With regard to the position of the various colours in the aura, the yellow of intellect, the rose of affection and the blue of devotion are always found in the upper part of the astral body. The colours of selfishness, avarice, deceit and hatred are in the lower part, whilst the mass of sensual feelings usually floats between the two.[1]

Changing the Aura

The aura can be subjected to the control of the will. Theosophy teaches that we can change our nature, and therefore our auras, just as we can the expression of our faces, and that both the superphysical and the physical changes are produced by thought. Harmonious [2] and outward-turned thoughts and feelings beautify and expand the aura. Discordant and self-centred thoughts deform it and make it ugly. As high ideals are followed and one's life becomes more and more purified from selfishness, the whole aura grows brighter, larger, more radiant. This evidence of evolutionary advancement would seem to be implied in the beautiful text: " The path of the just is as the shining light, that shineth more and more unto the perfect day." [3]

[1] For fuller information upon this subject see *Man, Visible and Invisible* by C. W. Leadbeater, from which the above information has been taken.

[2] One assurance of happines is to be harmonious and always to act as a harmoniser.

[3] *Prov.* IV. 18.

CHAPTER IV

THE ACTIVITY OF THE SOUL WHILST THE BODY SLEEPS

Precognition

DREAMS of action at a distance, of participation in events which prove actually to have happened, constitute very strange human experiences. Sometimes one dreams correctly of future events or receives warnings of danger should a certain action or journey be taken. Some people tell of dreaming correctly the numbers of winning lottery tickets or the names of winning racehorses. Such true premonitions can even be experienced whilst one is wide awake. To the enquiring mind such happenings present an intriguing problem. How can events become known when they are distant either in space or in time?

Astral Travel

Theosophy offers an explanation for these not uncommon experiences, teaching that man has an independent life quite apart from his physical body. When we fall asleep the Spiritual Self or Soul, robed in a body built of substance finer than physical gaseous matter, is able to move about the superphysical worlds and to pursue a life of its own in those realms. It is, in fact, possible to render service, both to deceased individuals who have died in distressing circumstances and to the sick and sorrowful who are still on earth.

Some years ago, when broadcasting on such subjects from Station 2GB, Sydney, Australia, I received many letters describing dreams which proved to be true records of events. Amongst many others, a lady from Perth, Western Australia, wrote saying that she had dreamt that she was floating over Sydney Harbour and had seen the famous Bridge, then newly completed, and a ship on fire coming in through the Heads. She knew that the fire would be subdued and the ship safely docked, but she failed in her efforts to convey this knowledge to the passengers, some of whom were much afraid. The shock sent her " flying ", as one sometimes does in dreams, right across Australia and back into her body, causing her to awaken deeply disturbed. She aroused her husband, related her dream, and they both noted the time. Next day the news showed that exactly at that time a ship on fire—with frightened passengers—had actually entered the Heads, just as she had dreamed. Fortunately, the fire was extinguished and the ship was safely docked. Quite evidently the lady, in her astral body, had travelled across Australia, witnessed the dramatic events of which she dreamed and, on returning to her body, had brought the memory to her brain.

The Divine Healer of Men

Here is a case of a *waking* vision in which a promise given was later fulfilled. Late one evening a New Zealand lady of my acquaintance was awaiting the passing of her young son who, according to the doctor, was not likely to live through the night. About midnight a Personage, whom she referred to as the Lord Jesus, entered the room in a physical form, accompanied by two men. After spending some time beside the unconscious body, the Lord turned towards her and said that her son had been healed and would live. This proved to be quite true, for that boy is alive to this day.

"Follow Me"

Another true story of a waking vision was told to me personally by the lady concerned, an honoured figure in Western Australia. One day a young English girl of aristocratic birth, on the threshold of a life full of happiness and opportunities, saw One whom she thereafter came to regard as her Master walking towards her across the lawn of her home in England. As she spontaneously knelt before Him, He asked her if she would dedicate her life to His service. She assented at once, entered an Order, and eventually received and answered a call to devote her whole life to helping aboriginal and other children in Western Australia, where she was known as Sister Kate. Throughout her long mission she was frequently conscious of her Master's support and Presence. She died a few years ago, but her great work for children goes on.

Accounts of such cases could be multiplied almost indefinitely. According to Theosophy they occur as a result of the power of the Soul of man—and especially of superhuman Beings, as in the last two cases—to travel, to be aware of and to act at a distance from the sleeping or entranced physical body. Theosophy teaches that whilst the forms of Nature and of man are subject to phases of becoming, development, maturity and disappearance, the Life within all forms is continuously existent. Similarly, the Inner Self or Ego of man is relatively everlasting. When once that Spiritual Soul has attained to conscious self-awareness, it neither sleeps nor dies. It is man's physical body that is impermanent; it both sleeps and dies. The Inner Self experiences no such break in its awareness. With varying faculties and powers, it is active on the mental and astral planes during bodily sleep.

Invisible Helping

Interesting examples of this process have reached me from a correspondent—not a Theosophist—in the South Island of New Zealand, who writes in effect: "I have long made it the last thought in my mind before sleeping to go to people whom I heard were ill, and in a number of instances, on waking, I have brought back the recollection of contacting them out of the body. Many times I have consciously left the body in the daytime and have seen my wife at the place where she is employed. By correctly describing her actions, I have proved to her that I had really seen her.

"A few months ago a local man was drowned and life pronounced extinct by the doctor at about 8.45 p.m. At 9 p.m. my wife and I retired, not knowing anything about this. I was no sooner in bed than I fell asleep and suddenly found myself facing this man, who was rather bewildered and in a reclining position. I said to him, 'You must realise that you have passed away from earthly life.' He replied: 'I am dead, then?' I said, 'Yes, but you must now go onwards and upwards.' He still looked bewildered, so I said 'Think of God.' He then began to float slowly upwards and the thought passed through my mind, 'Now he understands.' When I went on duty at 8 a.m. the following morning, the first thing that I was told was of this man's death by drowning."

In later conversation with the writer of these accounts, I became convinced both of his honesty and of the reality to him of these and other superphysical experiences which he described. Here is another of his typical descriptions, dated the 28th February, 1950: "On one occasion I found myself in the cockpit of a large plane and standing on the right side of the pilot. There were one or two other men in the background, but my attention was concentrated on the pilot. The inside of the cockpit appeared to be gloomy. I then heard a voice say, 'We are losing height.' The pilot did not answer, but I read his unspoken thought: 'I know.' Then, as I looked through the windscreen in front of the pilot, I noticed the same gloominess ahead of us and also saw, about a quarter of a mile away, a clump of trees towards which we were heading very rapidly and fast losing height. We appeared to be below the level of the tops of the trees, when the pilot at the last moment put the plane's nose upward at a very steep angle, to try and clear them; this failed and the plane seemed to strike the trees. There was a terrible crash on the bottom of the plane, and there my vision ended. I brought the idea back to waking consciousness that this had happened in Australia, and I found that aboriginals were also in my thoughts.

"Now comes the sequel. Eight days later—the 8th of March, 1950—I heard in the Australian Radio News Service an account of the crash of a Lincoln Bomber. The plane was seen coming down out of the clouds, losing height very rapidly. Unable to clear a clump of trees in its path, it crashed into them, bursting into flames. The four airmen were killed in this accident, which took place at Rosewood, Brisbane, Australia!"

Everyone may Learn to Help and Heal

Such instances could be continued almost indefinitely and Theosophy, whilst explaining them as representing real experiences of the Soul while away from the body during sleep, also tells how the faculties of astral travel and invisible helping may be developed. If, for example, during waking life, service has its increasing part in one's motives and actions, then—almost automatically—the same spirit of service will display itself when the Soul is freed from the body.

The best way to become an invisible helper is, in fact, to be a visible helper. If, in addition, a firm mental decision is made before falling to sleep at night that study and service will be carried out during the hours of bodily sleep, the resolve is taken that memory of such activity shall be brought through on waking and the practice of regular, wisely directed, daily meditation is followed, then fairly soon strong evidence, if not proof, of such out-of-the-body activity is likely to be obtained. Further information on this fascinating subject is available in modern Theosophical literature. *Invisible Helpers*, by C. W. Leadbeater, is strongly recommended to those who are interested.

PART TWO

MAN'S UNFOLDMENT TO PERFECTION THROUGH MANY EARTHLY LIVES

CHAPTER I

OBJECTIONS TO REINCARNATION ANSWERED

The Doctrine of Rebirth and the Western Mind

Belief in reincarnation is almost universal throughout the Orient. Although the doctrine is gradually gaining acceptance in the West, many people object strongly to the idea. Are these objections valid? Is there an alternative theory which explains human experience with equal logic? Does the absence of the teaching from orthodox Christianity constitute a weakness? Let us look at these problems together.

An Open Mind

The doctrine of reincarnation has a large place in the Theosophical philosophy of life. Perhaps an adequate description of it would be human evolution to perfection by means of successive lives on earth.

While this idea makes a strong appeal to some people, many of us feel the need for some kind of proof that the doctrine is really true. Such an inquiry must, of course, be approached with a completely open mind, for prejudice is one of the greatest barriers to the attainment of knowledge. Is it not a curious fact that whilst from time immemorial Oriental peoples have accepted reincarnation in one form or another as a basic and unchallengeable fact of life, we of the West hesitate to assent? In order to facilitate unprejudiced examination of the doctrine of rebirth, I will first consider some prevalent objections and then offer answers to each of them.

"We" do not Reincarnate

One of the commonest objections to reincarnation arises from a shrinking from life in the flesh, and from the suffering which is man's lot at this stage of human evolution. "I don't want to come back here again", so many people say. "Once is enough for me!" One cannot but sympathise with those whose experience of life has been so unfortunate as to bring them to such a conclusion. Nevertheless, according to the doctrine of reincarnation the objection is invalid, is misconceived; for by rebirth is not implied the return to earth of our present selves. *We* do not reincarnate. This personal self with its bodily and mental characteristics, its name, race, creed, sex and outlook—this person does not reincarnate.

Theosophy teaches that at death the temporary, mortal body is finally laid aside to reappear no more, and later on this also becomes true for the bodies of emotion and of mind. That which down here we generally regard as ourselves is not, in reality, our true

Selves at all. The real Self of man is an eternal, immortal, spiritual being, quite distinct from the physical body. Being immortal and eternal, it does not, cannot, die. The body, on the other hand, being but mortal, inevitably passes away. Since it had a beginning, it must have an end. The Spiritual Self is permanent, everlasting; never having had a beginning, it can never have an end. This all-important truth is beautifully expressed in Sir Edwin Arnold's poetic translation of the great Hindu Scripture, the *Bhagavad Gita*:

> " Never the spirit was born; the spirit shall cease to be never;
> Never was time it was not; End and Beginning are dreams!
> Birthless and deathless and changeless remaineth the spirit for ever;
> Death hath not touched it at all, dead though the house of it seems! " [1]

According to the doctrine of reincarnation it is the immortal, pilgrim God *within* the body which reincarnates, and not the mortal, bodily man with his transient feelings and thoughts. When, therefore, we think and say in objection to rebirth, " I do not want to return ", we need have no fear. We, as we normally know ourselves, do not return. It is the Divine Essence, the Spiritual Self with its acquired, individual attributes, which reincarnates.

[1] *The Song Celestial*, Sir Edwin Arnold.

Rebirth as Animals

A further objection is based upon the possibility that reincarnation might imply transmigration of Souls from human into animal forms. This is an entirely erroneous view of the doctrine and consequently, as an objection, is invalid. When once the Life in any form has attained to a certain level of unfoldment, although there may be delay or digression there is no real retrogression. Men are not reborn as animals.

Reunion

The mind may also shrink from accepting the idea of reincarnation on the ground that rebirth will so separate loved ones as to preclude all possibility of future reunion. This objection, in its turn, is invalid. Neither birth nor death nor rebirth can ever completely and finally separate those between whom a deep and strong spiritual, intellectual, or physical bond has been formed. In their Spiritual Selves, wherein the closest affinity has been established, those who love are for ever at one, whether physically embodied or disembodied. In the state of consciousness in which the Spiritual Self of man abides, painful separation is impossible, parting is unknown.

Furthermore, the very fact of the existence of so close a bond will cause those who love to descend repeatedly into incarnation at about the same time, and under conditions in which they are likely to meet. They will be drawn together by their affinity and by the law of cause and effect. On meeting again, although the new brain, the seat of memory, may not remember the incidents of past intimate associations, the heart speaks, a mutual attraction is felt and love is renewed—sometimes, indeed, at first sight. Once more a close relationship, differing in character in various incarnations, is established. This may be parental, filial, fraternal, or between comrades and colleagues. In each new association love deepens, grows more unselfish, more noble, until at last the state is reached of love perfected, which is life itself perfected.

Memory Preserved

Another objection to reincarnation is based upon the apparent absence of all memory of past lives. A little reflection will show, however, that recollection of the process of education is in no sense essential to possession of the acquired knowledge and faculty. We do not need to remember the processes of learning to walk, talk, read and write, in order to be able to do these things. Similarly, the absence of memory of incidents and experiences in past lives does not prevent the use of the resultant powers in later incarnations. Actually, the reincarnating Ego *does* retain both the full memory of all incidents of past life cycles and all the capacities attained. Furthermore, just as remembrance of childish struggles when learning to walk, talk, read and write is rarely retained in adult life, so recollection of the multifarious educative experiences of numerous preceding lives is not generally permitted to descend into the new mind-brain. In consequence, the weight of the drama of previous existences is withheld and the mind is left free to investigate and to assimilate new ideas.

This withholding of memory may have been implied in classical references to the River Lethe in the after-death world, the waters of which, when bathed in, gave forgetfulness of the past. The fruits of former lives are, however, expressed in each new personality as instinct and inherent " gifts ", as sympathies and antipathies, and as the voice of conscience.

Further evidence is to be found in many proven accounts of accurate memory of earlier lives. In certain cases such memories are true, and thereby constitute strong additional evidence in support of the idea of rebirth.

Regression of Memory

Whilst the only final proof of the truth of reincarnation consists of direct knowledge of one's own past lives, convincing evidence is provided by Colonel de Rochas in his book, *Les Vies Successives*. Therein he describes experiments with various sensitives put into a trance state by hypnotism. By the process known as regression of memory the operators succeeded in taking their subjects back to former incarnations, thus obtaining details—often of an historical character—which, when checked, were found to be entirely correct.

In one typical instance the sensitive chosen for an experiment was a young servant girl, with little or no education and but a rudimentary knowledge of history. When led back to a preceding life, she described correctly and with a wealth of detail historical events, little-known incidents, ancient customs and other matters of which she was completely ignorant in her present incarnation.

Recorded instances of children who in full waking consciousness remember details of their past lives, possess an even greater evidential value. These cases for the most part deal with children who, dying in their early years, are almost immediately reborn, thus making more likely the recollection of their last lives.

So it is that certain fundamental objections to the doctrine of rebirth are, on examination, found to be without much substance and need not in the least prevent acceptance of the idea of rebirth on purely logical grounds.

CHAPTER II

TRUE MEMORIES OF FORMER LIVES ON EARTH

Is Memory a Reliable Guide?

Do supposed memories of former lives justify belief in reincarnation? Such memories are far more common than is generally realised. When one begins to examine the doctrine of reincarnation critically and to search for evidence for and against it, one finds numbers of recorded instances of clear recollection of former lives which have been susceptible of test, and proved or disproved by means of historical records.

A Love Story of Ancient Egypt and its Modern Sequel

"An officer in the Indian Army remembered distinctly being a high official in the Court of one of the Pharaohs. He fell in love with a dancing girl, but the disparity of their social positions made marriage so far impossible. So they fled one night into the Theban desert, and had hardly got clear of the city before they were overtaken by a sandstorm. Before he could wrap her burnous round her mouth and nose, the sand enveloped them and they were both suffocated. Often and often did he have the old feeling of choking, as though repeating this supreme incident in the past. But he never met the girl. One night he was at a conversazione of the Royal Society, knowing no one (as he thought), when, looking round, he saw a girl leaning against the wall, staring at him. Something impelled him to move towards her, and he did so, and she simultaneously moved towards him across the room. When she reached him, she put out both her hands and said, 'Suffocated!' 'What!' he said, 'Do *you* remember?' 'Yes, indeed,' she said, 'and how you tried to wrap my scarf round my mouth.' They are married now."[1]

Here are three accounts of apparently proven memories of former lives.[2]

Legal Recognition

The first is the story of a certain Mansour Atrash. "It is vouched for by dozens of persons in the Djebel. This Mansour Atrash married a girl of twelve, by the name of Ummrumman, Mother of the Pomegranate. Shortly afterward he was killed in a raid. Those events occurred about thirty years ago. At the exact hour of his death, a fact afterward verified, there was

[1] *Vide Studies in the Lesser Mysteries*, The Rev. F. G. Montague Powell, M.A. The Theosophical Publishing Society, 161 New Bond St., W. London.

[2] *Vide Reincarnation, Fact or Fallacy?*, Geoffrey Hodson, T. P. H., Adyar, Madras, India.

born to a family of Druses hundreds of miles away, in the mountains of the Lebanon, a boy, whom they named Najib Abu Faray. He grew to be twenty years of age without ever leaving his native mountains, and then by accident was taken to the Djebel Druse, the old home of Mansour Atrash. As soon as he reached the Mountain, he said: 'I must be in a dream. I have seen all these places before; they are more familiar than my own mountains.' When he came to the village in which Mansour Atrash had lived, he said: 'This is my village, and my house is up a certain street and on a certain corner.' He walked through the twisting streets, straight to a walled-up recess, had the bricks torn down, and discovered a small bag of money that he remembered having put there in his former life. Later he was taken to some vineyards belonging to the Atrash family, where there were disputed boundaries. He pointed out the boundaries that he said he had laid when he was Mansour Atrash, and a Druse court of law accepted them. He had now given so many proofs of his identity that he was recognised by the children of Mansour Atrash as their reincarnated father, and received ten camel-loads of grain as a present from the Atrash family."

An Indian Case

The second account is as follows: "In the latter half of 1922, a three-year-old Indian boy named Vishwa Nath, of Bareilly, India, surprised his parents by giving them minute details of what he claimed was his previous life. The boy pestered his father about a place called Pilibhit, wanting to know how far it was from Bareilly, and begging his father to take him there. His father and mother, believing [quite erroneously] that children with such memories die young, tried everything in their power to make the boy forget his strange fancies. But as he grew older his preoccupation with his past life grew more intense. Yielding to the boy's entreaties, his parents took him to the Government High School in Pilibhit. The boy said he did not recognise the school. It was, in fact, a new building.

"Vishwa Nath then astounded his hearers with a wealth of information about his previous life in Pilibhit. He said his neighbour had been a Lafa-Sunder Lal, who boasted a green gate, a sword and a gun, and who held nautch parties in the courtyard of his house. He said his father had been a landowner with a great fondness for wine, rohu fish and nautch girls. He claimed that he had studied in the Government school, passing in Urdu, Hindi and English, and reaching the sixth class. All this was subsequently confirmed as correct. He described the house in which he had lived, including its interior, and when taken to the building everything was found exactly as he described it, including the position of a staircase. The little boy put his finger correctly upon a man in a group photograph as being Har Narai, finally capping his amazing memory of another life by pointing to himself—a boy seated in a chair. The boy in the photograph was Laxmi Narain, son of Babu Nai Narain, who had died of lung trouble at Shajehuenpur, on December 15, 1918, at the age of thirty-two. Among other details given correctly by Vishwa Nath were the exact site of class six in the local school, the appearance of his teacher, the names of places where he had worked and the name of his personal servant. The boy's maternal uncle corroborated many of these statements, including facts everyone else had forgotten."

Marionettes

Here is the third story. "He, Fielding Hall . . . vouches for the case of a little girl of seven who told him in detail the story of her previous incarnation, in which she said she had been a man who ran a marionette show. To test her, her parents brought her a marionette doll. She at once manipulated the strings quite correctly, although she had never seen a marionette before. 'I have been married four times,' she said. 'Two of my wives died, one I divorced, and one was living when I died, and is living still. I loved her very much indeed. The one I divorced was a very dreadful woman.' Pointing to a scar on her shoulder, she added: 'See this? She took up a chopper and cut me.'

"Fielding Hall made some inquiries and found that a birth-mark on the child corresponded exactly to a mark which had been given to a former owner of a marionette show by his wife, who had been traced. The divorced wife and the much-loved wife were still living, and when asked why she did not go to live with the 'wife' she loved so much, the little girl replied: 'But that was all in a former life.' In addition, the child accurately described places and people living great distances away that she had never seen and had known only in her previous life."

Instinct as Memory

Admittedly, physical remembrance of incidents of past lives is rare, but of memory as far as innate capacity and knowledge are concerned there is complete evidence in both the animal and the human kingdoms of Nature. One Theosophical explanation of animal instinct is that it is a form of recollection. The soul, or consciousness, evolving through ducklings, for example, has evolved through other ducks in earlier times and knows instinctively that ducks can swim. In the new brain the ducklings do not remember those previous existences, but they have brought over the instinct which results from them and so, quite naturally, they swim. All instinctive habits and customs in the animal kingdom are similarly attributable to race memory.

Domestic animals often repeat old habits which belonged to their earlier phases of evolution, when they were still in a wild state. The dog will frequently turn round and round before he lies down because in earlier days, as wolf, he had need to tread down his jungle or forest bed in order to make it comfortable. Like the duckling, he does not remember the incidents but follows his instinct, even though in his case the need for the action no longer exists.

The Origin of Human Relationships

In much the same instinctive fashion we human beings " remember " our past lives. Our inherent " gifts "—actually hard-won faculties—our natural sympathies and our antipathies are remembrances of the past. Love at first sight—that love which springs suddenly into existence and may last for a lifetime—is but the spontaneous renewal of an ancient tie. There are others for whom we feel an inborn aversion which also has its roots in other lives, when the relationship was not a happy one. We thus bring with us into each new incarnation intuitive rather than detailed memory of old associations. The fruits of these experiences manifest themselves in the new personality as innate faculties, sympathies and antipathies which would otherwise be difficult to explain.

CHAPTER III

THE MYSTERY OF CHILD PRODIGIES SOLVED BY REINCARNATION

Whence Comes Genius?

WHAT is the explanation of talents and unusually gifted people? How do children come to possess and display with ease mental powers, artistic faculties and physical genius far beyond those of their elders who have studied and practised for half a lifetime?

The Everlasting Arms

Before offering a Theosophical explanation of child prodigies, I wish to quote a truly Theosophical utterance by Horace Bushwell who said: "Every human soul has a complete and perfect plan cherished for it in the heart of God—a divine biography marked out which it enters into life to live. This life, rightly unfolded, will be a complete and beautiful whole, an experience led on by God and unfolded by His secret nurture, as are the trees and flowers by the secret nurture of the world. We live in the Divine thought. We fill a place in the everlasting plan of God's intelligence. We never sink below His care—never drop out of His counsel."

Even if we do go wrong—betray the pattern at times through ignorance—God, Life, Law (or however the Deity may be conceived) brings us back to the right road again and somehow makes use of our error. A Persian aphorism says: "God writes straight on crooked lines."

Remarkable Children

Let us now turn to a perplexing human problem—that of infant prodigies. Here is a real story of one of them, published in the New Zealand Press on December 13th, 1950.

"*Uncanny Infant Prodigies*: A new Datas—aged three and three-quarters—is astounding English interviewers by the ease with which he reads Shakespeare, newspapers, novels, fairy tales and magazines, remembers telephone numbers and counts up to one thousand. The name of this youthful wizard is Jonathan Richard Cocking, who lives with his father and mother in Hendon, north-west London. Jonathan reads his newspapers regularly, including the Korean war news.

"A lot of tests have been tried out on Jonathan to see if the claims made for him are genuine, and he has passed them all with flying colours. He can do crossword puzzles and beat his pals at games, including snakes and ladders, and yet he is a normally behaved, jolly child, who looks upon his own prowess as he would upon a joke or a game.

"Jonathan's father is a research engineer and his mother was once a secretary. Jonathan taught himself to read, write and add. In fact, his parents discouraged him because they were afraid he would overtax his strength. His memory is really incredible. He could talk when he was ten months old, *and was really a fluent conversationalist at twelve months old.* His mother says: 'He is mad about buses, and his craze for them spurred him on because he wanted to understand all about tickets, destinations and numbers.'

" 'Jonathan went on a holiday to Wales this summer. He learnt to reel off Welsh names before we had been there for a week,' said his father. 'He has a bad habit of correcting adults' grammar. Some of my Cockney friends don't like it.

" 'Jonathan at three years nine months old weighs 3st. 2½lbs. and is 3ft. 8in. tall. When he is not reading aloud for tests at fifty words a minute, he amuses himself by playing with his toy dogs and writing in his writing book or learning the telephone numbers of friends, neighbours and tradesmen. He never makes an error. But,' says his father, 'Jonathan is no prig.' "

What can be the explanation of these and similar remarkable powers displayed by very young people? Why did Sir William Hamilton at the age of thirteen know thirteen different languages, when it takes an ordinary man several years to master any one of them? Why should Mozart and so many others show in early childhood musical and artistic powers that many of us cannot hope to attain after lifelong work? Why should Alan Leo, without any previous study, take with ease to astrology, a subject that is known to tax the keenest intelligence?

Faculty Preserved and Re-expressed

The explanation offered by Theosophy of the phenomenal powers displayed so early in life is that the Inner Self, the true individuality behind the bodily veil, sometimes called the Ego, has concentrated on those studies in former lives. This concentration has enabled these individuals to master both the theory and the technique of such subjects, and they are born with an instinctive knowledge or natural flair in those directions. Heredity is not, cannot be, a satisfactory explanation; for very often an examination of the parentage and earlier ancestry of a genius fails to reveal the presence of special aptitudes which could explain the youthful precocity and virtuosity of their gifted descendant.

Musical Genius

Take Mozart, for example. Here is an announcement which appeared in a German newspaper in 1763, advertising an appearance of the boy Mozart.

"Positively the last concert! . . . The boy, not yet seven, will perform on the harpsichord, play a concerto for violin, and accompany symphonies on the clavier, the keyboard being covered with a cloth, as easily as if he could see the keys. He will name all notes sounded at a distance, singly or in chords, and improvise on harpsichord and organ as long as desired."

Thus the most universal genius of music the world has ever known, Wolfgang Amadeus Mozart, was advertised as if he were a side-show freak. Another boy, the fourteen-year-old Goethe, also destined to become immortal, was in the audience at that performance. Years later Goethe could still recall the far-off, bright picture of the merry-faced little musician who ran to the bench before the harpsichord in his absurd, exquisite costume of lilac satin with powdered wig and tiny sword, and played with such mastery and verve.

Mozart was born with an inexplicably (reincarnation apart) complete gift. He possessed absolute pitch, infallible rhythm and natural comprehension of harmony. Thus, at the age of four the child began to learn to play the clavier, a forerunner of the modern piano, and at five picked up a violin and, reading at sight, managed to play through six trios with his father and a friend. He read and wrote notes before he could do as much with letters. Compositions dating even from his sixth year display the unique characteristics which later came to be recognised as peculiar to the music of Mozart.

An Italian Prodigy

Here is another example of a child prodigy, published in *The New Zealand Herald* of March 2nd, 1948: "The eight-year-old Italian conductor, Ferruccio Burgo, made a triumphant debut with a symphony orchestra at the Carnegie Hall in New York. The curly-headed boy in knee pants showed no signs of nervousness as he conducted an eighty-piece orchestra in five Operatic Overtures and Beethoven's First Symphony. Professional critics praised his good sense of rhythm, notable musical memory and feeling for melody. He first conducted publicly at Fiume at the age of four."

One readily sees how the doctrine of reincarnation solves the problem which child prodigies propound. Their strange genius has been brought over from former lives, in which mastery of their subjects was attained. In a new life, in consequence of their previous achievements, they merited a parentage and a body through which their acquired genius could be expressed. Thereafter, if such is the plan of the new life, they display their unusual faculties, and often whilst still quite young.

* * * *

(A fuller exposition of this subject will be found in my book *Reincarnation, Fact or Fallacy?*, from which part of the material for this broadcast was taken.)

PART THREE

LIFE IS RULED BY LAW

CHAPTER I

THE LAW OF CAUSE AND EFFECT ASSURES JUSTICE TO EVERY HUMAN BEING

Is There Justice for Man?

In this broadcast we are going to consider some basic problems of human life and their Theosophical solutions. All thoughtful people, on occasion, find themselves perplexed by the difficulties, the apparent futility and the seeming injustice of common human experience.

Here, for example, are five such problems: first, the place of apparent accident in life; second, fair play, justice, in human affairs; third, infant prodigies; fourth, death, bereavement and reunion after death; and fifth, the dual problem of man's happiness and the means of reducing to a minimum his sorrows and sicknesses.

Sowing and Reaping

One general answer may be offered to all human problems; it is the existence and operation in life of the law of cause and effect, action and reaction, or compensation, as Emerson called it. This causative sequence is regarded, Theosophically, as the one decisive force in human affairs. Under the law of cause and effect, each one of us makes or mars his own life by his own conduct. All conditions and all experiences are self-produced under the operation of this law, which St. Paul describes in these words: "God is not mocked: for whatsoever a man soweth, that shall he also reap." [1] Our Lord referred to the law of causation, to its immutability, and to the exactitude of its operation, in such sayings as: "For verily I say unto you, Till heaven and earth pass, one jot or one tittle shall in no wise pass from the law, till all be fulfilled." [2] And again: "Judge not, that ye be not judged. For with what judgment ye judge, ye shall be judged: and with what measure ye mete, it shall be measured to you again." [3] Theosophy also teaches of this law and in doing so stands each individual on his own feet, shows him as the decreer of his own glory and the maker of his own gloom.

The Life Story of Abraham Lincoln

Let me now apply this doctrine to the first of our five problems, that of apparent accidents in human life. In illustration, take the story of the rise to fame and the death by assassination of Abraham Lincoln. This was one of the most fateful occurrences in the history of the U. S. A., of the Negro people and,

[1] *Gal.* VI. 7.
[2] *Matt.* V. 18.
[3] *Ibid.*, VII. 1-2.

indeed, of the whole world. Yet four seemingly chance events made Abraham Lincoln President of the U. S. A.

He was a disappointed and discouraged lawyer in the Middle West. In 1860 the failure of his son, Robert, in the Harvard Entrance Examination caused Lincoln to travel to New York, and then to Connecticut. This failure of his son to pass the Examination was the first apparent chance happening in Lincoln's rise to fame; for when it was known that he was passing through New York City, an invitation was sent to him to deliver a lecture there—the second event in the arranging of which he had no part. He held the vast meeting spellbound by his logic, and at its close the audience broke into wild and prolonged enthusiasm. This led to many further engagements, and to Lincoln being regarded as a possible candidate for nomination for President of the U. S. A. by the Republican Party.

The third event arose from the second incident. A certain Richard J. Oglesby of Decatur, a Republican politician, became moved by a sudden sense of showmanship. He remembered that Lincoln and John Hanks, another Republican, in their youth had split rails on a farm. In those pioneer days railsplitting was a sign that a man had his roots deep in American soil. At the Republican Convention of 1860, John Hanks appeared on the stage carrying the very rails these two men had split ten years before, in 1850. On the rails was a large sign: "Abraham Lincoln, the Rail Splitter, candidate for President 1860." The

Convention went wild. "Abe Lincoln, the Rail Splitter" became a national slogan. He was nominated but his better known opponent, Seward, was greatly favoured and on a preliminary test vote defeated Lincoln.

Then came the fourth apparent accident. The voting papers for the official polling, which had been promised by the printer by 9 p.m. did not arrive till next morning! That printer became the instrument of destiny for, seizing their opportunity, Lincoln's friends went feverishly to work. By next morning they had changed public opinion and Lincoln secured the Republican nomination. Later in the year 1861 he was elected sixteenth President of the U. S. A. and was re-elected in 1864.

Life is Ruled by Law

Thus, apparent chance decided the fate and development of both Lincoln and the American people. He later delivered his famous anti-slavery pronouncement, which led to the Civil War of 1861-1865 and to the freeing of thousands of slaves. Lincoln was assassinated in 1865 by John Wilkes Booth. So ended a very great career founded upon apparent accidents, or at least upon events which Lincoln did not himself initiate.

Perfect Justice Assured to Every Human Being

Was it all mere chance, or was some principle in operation under which strict justice was being meted out to Abraham Lincoln? No, it was not mere chance. Strict justice was, in fact, being done. In former lives on earth Lincoln had so acted that the events of his Nineteenth Century life were practically inevitable. Theosophy teaches that mere chance is impossible. Not even the smallest injustice can ever occur to any human being or Nation. Everything that happens either to an individual or to a Nation is an effect, a reaction, caused by a preceding, originating action.

The Karma[1] of Nations

In the case of Nations, the causative action can generally be discovered in that Nation's history. Germany, for example, pursued the policy of wanton aggression from the time of Frederick I. For a time she succeeded but, after the Kaiser and Hitler had carried out that policy with still greater effrontery, Germany went down to defeat. In the case of the individual person, the cause must have been set going either in the present or in a preceding life on earth, for an exact, invariable, inviolable law operates upon all human beings. Under this law, effects follow causes as surely as night follows day.

A Human Tragedy

Let us now apply these ideas to another strange story of a human experience. In December 1950, a Melbourne Criminal Court acquitted a mother living at Carnegie on a charge of murdering her daughter, aged 19. Evidence was that, in a nightmare, Mrs. Cogdon dreamt that Korean soldiers were attacking her daughter,

[1] *Karma* (*Sk.*), the law of cause and effect.

Patricia, in the girl's bedroom. Sleep-walking, she rose, took an axe, went to the girl's room and struck several times at the imaginary figure of a soldier on the bed. The girl died from blows on the side of the head. The jury gave its verdict without waiting for Counsels' addresses. Legal men said that to their knowledge a plea of somnambulism had never been used before as a successful defence against a murder charge.

Here, again, we see destiny at work. It was within the bounds of perfect justice that, because of deeds in a former life, the daughter should meet this strange end. It was not, however, within the bounds of strict justice that her mother, who murdered her during her own sleep, should suffer the death penalty or even be punished at all by a Court, deeply though she must have suffered and must still be suffering on account of her unconscious act.

Law or Capricious Chance?

One more story, a strange footnote to history, was recorded in the New Zealand Press in December, 1950, as follows: "New Plymouth won first prize in the 'Prizes for Xmas' Art Union, drawn today. Three of the other four major prizes went to the Auckland province. Major prize-winner was: £2000—Brian English, 3 years old." Just think of the potential influence on that child's life, on his education and on his future career, as well as upon the rest of the family, produced by the apparent chance winning of a lottery when only three years old!

The Purpose of Human Experience

As I understand Theosophy, the Carnegie mother and her daughter, and three-year-old Brian English and his family, were all doing two things. They were working out the destiny formed by their own actions in past lives, and they were also influencing their future incarnations. Apart from the operation of the law of cause and effect, man is granted a measure of freedom of will, thought and conduct. By the use which he makes of his freedom, he largely decides the manner in which his destiny will be fulfilled. That destiny itself is, however, fixed. It is evolution to perfection or, as it was defined by St. Paul, " Till we all come in the unity of the faith, and of the knowledge of the Son of God, unto a perfect man, unto the measure of the stature of the fulness of Christ." [1]

There is the goal of human life perfectly described —to come " unto the measure of the stature of the fulness of Christ." That is why we are here, that is the great deliverance to which we are all journeying, that is why we endure our manifold afflictions, experience our upliftments and our joys; for all these are the means whereby the Divine powers, potentially present in the Soul of man from the beginning, germinate and develop from the seed-like state to full unfoldment.

If you will think it over deeply, you will see that there are no alternatives to exact law and reincarnation save chaos, mere blind chance, in human affairs. The existence and operation from life to life of the law of

[1] *Eph.* IV. 13.

cause and effect alone can restore reason, meaning and purpose to human life.

A Scientific Philosophy of Life

The twin doctrines of causality in human affairs and of man's evolution to perfection through successive earthly lives are extremely important, and for two reasons. First, they provide a logical solution of otherwise insoluble problems and second, they make possible a belief, based on reason, in both assured justice and a noble destiny awaiting every man—namely, perfection of the power to help.

These two doctrines are indispensable to the mental peace of the humanitarian who is also a logician; for without reincarnation and the compensatory law, the ephemeral nature of human life and the inequalities of human experience pose a riddle which defies rational solution. Together, however, the two principles throw a flood of light upon man's existence. In that light his life can be fully comprehended from its inception, through its evolution, tribulations and happinesses, and on to its glorious goal.

Thus mentally illumined, and with courage born of reason, we can face the difficulties and trials of life; *for we know our own preceding hurtful actions to be their sole causes and that harmlessness to all creatures, including our own bodies, is their sure prevention.*

Looked at from this point of view the sufferings of mankind are rather like the tempest on Galilee,[1] without

[1] *Matt.* VIII. 23-27.

which the sleeping Christ might not have been awakened; for by their very stress the storms of human life awaken into action man's dormant Christ nature and powers. By employing these, he develops the capacity both to still the storms within himself and to render effective aid to his storm-tossed fellow men.

Reincarnation and *karma* thus provide an inspiring and logical philosophy of life, which may be simply stated in the following four postulates:

Perfected manhood is the assured destiny of the Spiritual Self of every man.

Reincarnation, as the evolutionary method, provides the necessary time and opportunity for self-perfecting.

The law of action and continually modified reaction ensures justice to all men.

The attainment of perfection is rendered certain by the interior presence of an infinite, Divine power ceaselessly at work within the Spiritual Self of every human being.

* * * * *

(A fuller exposition of this subject will be found in my book *Reincarnation, Fact or Fallacy?*, from which part of the material for this broadcast was taken.)

CHAPTER II

WAR OR PEACE, DEFEAT OR VICTORY, DECIDED BY PAST NATIONAL CONDUCT

THE PRINCIPLE OF COMPENSATION

Belgium Invaded, Switzerland Immune

THE history of Nations poses many problems. How was it, for example, that in the two World Wars of this century Belgium and France both suffered so heavily, whilst Sweden and Switzerland were immune? How was it that, whilst war raged all about these two countries, neither of them was drawn into the conflict? Why were Germany and Italy vanquished and their Dictators, Hitler and Mussolini, disgraced and execrated? What can there have been in the past of these and other Nations and people to explain such a strange diversity of experience in the midst of a general European conflagration?

The Karma of Nations

The subject is important, as I think you will see; for if we can find the root causes of the sufferings, the losses, the victories, and the defeats of some Nations in war and of the immunity, and even gain, of other Nations in the same war, then we shall possess both a key to national immunity from strife and knowledge of the way to world peace. According to Theosophy, that key is the existence and continual operation of the law of cause and effect.

Under this law Nations and their leaders create their own destiny and, largely by former actions, decide their own victories and defeats. Theosophy thus teaches that in both national and personal experience there is neither chaos nor chance. On the contrary, order and law everywhere prevail.

The Case of Germany

In the light of this affirmation of the existence of order and of law let us first consider Germany, which made itself an object of interest, as also of terror, to the Nations of the world. A study of her history reveals that in Germany we have an excellent example of the operation of the law of cause and effect. In the Eighteenth Century Frederick the Great initiated the national policy of unprovoked and wanton aggression. Temporarily he succeeded, gaining the addition of Silesia into German territory. Bismarck continued this course of action. He, too, found it to be temporarily profitable, having acquired Schleswig-Holstein and Alsace-Lorraine as a result. Unprovoked aggression had become part of German national policy. But when in 1914 William II, the Kaiser, pursued that same policy, he came to grief and brought disaster to the country. That, however, did not prevent Hitler from carrying it to a still higher pitch of effrontery and faithlessness, bringing still greater suffering to his country and defeat, world-wide execration and death to himself and many of his associates.

Thus, from the records of history we are able to observe the action of the law of causation. Wanton aggression inevitably brings national death and disintegration. Tyranny carries its own end within itself. Both constitute violations of natural as well as of Divine law. Both, therefore, bring their own nemesis, their inevitable punishment.

The Law of Cause and Effect

Before we proceed to examine the past history and later experiences of other countries, let me offer a fuller description of the law of compensation, or *karma*, the Sanskrit name by which it is known in the East. The word *karma* means action and is also used to connote both the operation of the law and its effects upon Nations and people. *Karma* is more fully described as the one universal law which guides unerringly all other laws under which effects follow causes. It is an incessant, impersonal adjustment, a cosmic attuning agency ceaselessly at work. It is not moral. It does not reward or punish in the personal sense, but re-attunes. Its influence is, however, both educative and morally corrective. The law " moves to righteousness " [1] and

[1] *The Light of Asia,* Sir Edwin Arnold, Book VIII. Perusal of this important and beautiful work is strongly advised.

operates upon man as cause and effect. Actions which disturb the harmony of the Universe provoke attunement. This is irresistible and can be painful, especially if resented and temporarily resisted. Actions which preserve, and restore when disturbed, the harmony of the Universe are in accord with Cosmic purpose and so result in happiness, moreness, fullness and growing freedom. *Be harmonious and live as a harmoniser*, then health, happiness and inward serenity will ultimately be assured to you.

Theosophy thus reveals both a profound secret of life and a way to happiness and health. Every great teacher has offered to mankind this doctrine of the law as a guide to conduct, an incentive to self-discipline and a solution to the problems of the apparent injustices of undeserved suffering and the inequalities of human birth and experience. Knowledge of *karmic* law, and especially of the principle of universal harmonisation upon which it rests, also reveals the way to world peace, for when a sufficient number of Nations and people become harmonious and harmonisers in thought, motive, word and deed, then world peace will reign on earth—and not before.

Karma in the Bible

Our Lord enunciated the doctrine of cause and effect many times during His ministry, as in the following quotations:

"For verily I say unto you, Till heaven and earth pass, one jot or one tittle shall in no wise pass from the law, till all be fulfilled." (*Matt*. V. 18.)

"And it is easier for heaven and earth to pass than one tittle of the law to fail." (*Luke* XVI. 17.)

"Judge not, that ye be not judged. For with what judgment ye judge, ye shall be judged: and with what measure ye mete, it shall be measured unto you again." (*Matt*. VII. 1, 2.)

"Therefore all things whatsoever ye would that men should do to you, do ye even so to them: for this is the law and the prophets." (*Matt*. VII. 12.)

In the Old Testament, also, we read:

"Whoso sheddeth man's blood, by man shall his blood be shed." (*Gen*. IX. 6.)

Thus we are taught that if we sow evil, selfishness, ugliness and cruelty by thought, word and deed, we shall reap accordingly. Conversely, if we sow beneficence, selflessness, beauty and kindliness we shall also reap the same.

We Modify Our Karma Continually

To the enunciation of this law of cause and effect must be added the principle of the modification of *karma* by the intervening actions performed before causes have had time to produce their full effects. Whatever one's actions in the past—good or bad in varying degrees—their reactions are not to be regarded as a dead, fixed weight from which there is no relief.

Both individuals and Nations, by their subsequent actions, are constantly modifying the operation upon themselves of the law of action and reaction. Thus, neither individuals nor Nations are ever paralysed by their former conduct. Everything is not irretrievably fated, however good or bad the past may have been. Man can master circumstances and make of each experience an opportunity for a fresh beginning, however heavily the past may weigh upon him.

In the light of these teachings, it becomes unmistakably clear that the "tides and tornadoes"[1] of world events and wars of our lifetime are not mere chance disasters. The failure of the League of Nations and of U. N. O. to prevent war is not to be regarded as mankind's undeserved ill-fortune. Under the law of cause and effect we, ourselves, are alone responsible for world conditions.

I am now going to test this idea of compensation by a study of the history of certain Nations; for it is, in fact, easier to discern the processes of action and reaction in the history of Nations than in the lives of individuals. National history is preserved and is available to the student. Past conduct can therefore be compared with later experiences and the whole teaching of the law of causation be put to the test. In the case of individuals, however, many of the major causes of present conditions and experiences were set going in former lives, and of those no easily available records exist.

[1] Winston Churchill.

The Importance of Knowledge of the Law

Whether information concerning the nature of such causative actions is available or not, knowledge of the existence and general mode of operation of the law of cause and effect is exceedingly important to mankind; for if everbody fully believed that appropriate reactions inevitably followed every action, then war would soon cease, crime would be greatly reduced and many other evils would disappear. No one who clearly understood the impersonality and inevitability of the sequence of cause and effect in human experience would dare by hurtful conduct to provoke the awful retaliation of the law. Action and its inevitable and appropriate reaction may, indeed, be regarded as part of the message of war to mankind. We cannot wage even economic warfare without sowing seeds of military strife, for both groups of people and Nations have collective *karma.* As communities we sow and reap, and individuals are sent to incarnate in Nations whose *karma* harmonises with their own. If, therefore, man desires peace and justice on earth he must think peace and justice, he must speak peace and justice and he must live in peace and be just. Otherwise U. N. O. will fail to prevent war, as did the League of Nations before it.

Such is the age-old and fundamental doctrine of the law of cause and effect, sowing and reaping, or *karma.* Such, in general, is its application to human conduct, experience and welfare.

Let us now try and discern the operation of this law upon Nations. As I embark upon this study of history in the light of *karma*, I would ask my readers to remember that when I refer to discordant and cruel actions of Nations I am neither criticising nor condemning. There is no ingredient of judgment in such realistic observation; for I believe that, in general, the peoples of the Nations of the world are kind and good, however mistaken their leaders may sometimes be. Neither are my deductions offered in the least dogmatically. Rather are they presented as ideas to be considered and as food for thought.

Why Belgium Suffered

Let us take Belgium, for example. Why did she suffer so heavily in the two World Wars? Can we find in her history aggressive conduct and wanton infliction of cruelty upon weaker peoples of such a nature and on such a scale as would seem to justify, according to the principle of cause and effect, her subsequent military disasters and the sufferings they brought to her people? Yes, I think we can. With every respect to noble Belgium, I would draw attention to what have come to be known by historians as "the Belgian Congo atrocities". I shall not describe in detail these products of the purely colonial administration of the Belgian Government of the time, but would refer those who are interested, and who wish to test the theory I am propounding, to the official records and photographs illustrating the barbarous treatment meted out to the indigenous population of the Belgian Congo colonies. From these it may reasonably be deduced that the Congo atrocities constituted a sowing from which the later national disasters were a not inappropriate reaping, to use the analogy of St. Paul.[1]

The Tribulations of France

France, to take another country, has three times been invaded and twice defeated and occupied by the Germans. Can we find deeds in earlier epochs which could be regarded justly as sowings from which later tribulations were the appropriate reapings? I think we can. For a long time, like Britain and other European Nations, France was one of the great feudal countries of Europe. For centuries royalty and aristocracy obtained their power and their wealth at the cost of the masses, including the large peasant population. Long continued exploitation and oppression were inflicted upon a poor and relatively helpless people. The massacre of the Hugenots on St. Bartholomew's Eve, 1572, was one of the most brutal of the many religious persecutions recorded in the history of Christendom. The royalty and the aristocracy of France had long been sitting upon the volcano of the bitterness and the rebellion of the masses. When this erupted, the French Revolution of 1789 broke out and the forces of brutality, bloodshed and barbarism were liberated. The Napoleonic Wars spread disaster and death throughout the many countries which Napoleon invaded. The terrible penal colony of French Guiana, known as Devil's Island, and the penal ships which

[1] *Gal.* VI. 7.

took the miserable victims thereto, were for a long time the cause of intense and widespread human misery.

Does it not seem reasonable to assume that from these sanguinary sowings the subsequent national tribulations were a natural reaping under the causative law? Indeed, it would seem permissible to conclude that in the case of France, as in that of Belgium, the operation of the law of cause and effect can be clearly discerned.

CHAPTER III

THE HISTORY OF SPAIN, PORTUGAL, SWITZERLAND AND BRITAIN IN THE LIGHT OF CAUSATIVE LAW

Do Nations Rise and Fall by Chance or according to Law?

WERE the defeat and subsequent downfall of Spain due to a caprice of the weather, or were deeper causes at work?

The Fall of Spain

The history of Spain has been a very dramatic one. In the Middle Ages this country was on the threshold of World Empire. She owned colonies in the Americas, the Philippines and the West Indies. She was enabled twice to build the greatest Armada the world had known up to that time. Then, almost in a night, her fall began. The great ships were wrecked on the shores of Britain, the very country she set out to defeat, for, as historians have said, " God sent a wind! " Truly, Drake, his ships and his men also contributed, but the storm of those days and nights admittedly played a large part in the defeat of the first Armada.

The Weather and History

If I may here digress for a moment, a study of the influence of the weather upon human history is full of interest. How strange that storms wrecked the Armada, whilst a calm upon the often turbulent English Channel permitted the evacuation of no less than 350,000 British soldiers from Dunkirk! Divine favouritism, could it be said? Or mere chance, might we presume? Neither, says Theosophy, but the impersonal operation of an exact law of cause and effect. Even the weather can be, and often is, as much an instrument of individual and national destiny as any other agency, including human enemies and friends—an interesting and intriguing thought.

The Armada defeated, Spain's decline was rapid. Soon afterwards she lost her colonies. In recent years she has been ravaged by a Civil War, and for a long time has not been considered worthy of admission to the family of Nations gathered together in U.N.O.—a decline, indeed, from a once proud position as a world power.

What is the explanation of this decline? In answer I would say: "Read the history of Spain; follow the *Conquistadores*, the conquerors, under Pizarro and Cortez, into Mexico and Peru and see how they and their soldiers treated the peoples of those countries." Spain's earlier treatment of the Moors and the Jews left much to be desired and she was long the home of one of the most brutal and cruel of all human institutions on earth, the Spanish Inquisition. This has played so important a part in the history of Europe, and has been so notable an example of the depths of sadistic cruelty and bigotry to which humanity can descend, that its origin and activities may usefully, if briefly, be considered at this point.

The Responsibility of Monarchs

The Spanish Inquisition was organised by Ferdinand V and Isabella, who appointed Tomas de Torquemada (1420-98) as Inquisitor-General of Castile and Aragon and charged him with the centralisation of the Spanish Inquisition in 1483. Isabella, a narrow-minded and bigoted Queen, impaired the strength and vitality of Spain by her religious persecutions. After the defeat of the Armada the Spaniards believed, or pretended to believe, that God had forsaken them because there was heresy in their midst. The supposed heretics were the Moriscoes, a dark-skinned race, half a million in number. Spain proceeded to expel these innocent people, thereby losing a large number of deserving, skilled agriculturalists and artisans. One of Queen Isabella's first acts on coming to the throne was to conquer Granada, which had hitherto been ruled by enlightened Moslems and was an oasis of culture, art, science and philosophy. The defeat of the Armada marked the decline of Spain for, proving that she was not invincible, it gave the Nations courage boldly to withstand her tyranny.

Inhuman Cruelty

The Spanish Inquisition was introduced by the Spaniards wherever they went and especially in America, the Spanish Netherlands and Naples, and had virtually the power of life and death over its victims. Inquisitors were infamous for their use of torture, and the harshness of many of the Spanish Courts brought the Inquisition into general opprobrium. Thus this country became the centre of widespread cruelty. Even today one of the most cruel of all blood sports, the bull fight, is a favoured national spectacle in Spanish countries. Indeed, in the case of Spain, also, it would seem that in the words of St. Paul: " God is not mocked; for whatsoever a man "—and here we might add, a Nation —" soweth, that shall he also reap." [1] For a time Spain prospered, but the seed of her decline was long present within her. Its name is cruelty. True, cruelty and tyranny succeeded for a time, but as an old proverb says " God (meaning law) permits; but not forever."

National Recovery

We have considered the past conduct and subsequent experiences of Germany, Belgium, France and Spain. Let us now look at Portugal, Switzerland and Britain. Portugal was at the height of its fame and prosperity during the years 1521 to 1527 under King John III. Then came the introduction of the Spanish Inquisition and all the horrors of cruelty which that Institution inflicted upon large numbers of people. Quite soon a national decline began. Portugal was conquered by Spain, with whom she later suffered. In 1750, however, she expelled the authors of the

[1] *Gal.* VI. 7

Inquisition and suspended its operations. Afterwards Portugal became a free, democratic country, honoured amongst the Nations of the world. As in the case of Spain, cruelty of an inhuman character was followed by national decline and, in Portugal's case, the extirpation of a cruel instrument was followed by an improvement in national affairs.

How Peace May be Assured

Switzerland's maintenance of neutrality in both the First and Second World Wars and her immunity from the sufferings, the casualties and the material destruction experienced by other European Nations, are especially notable. What is the explanation of this immunity? Has Switzerland been so philanthropic a member of the Family of Nations, and so benign in her internal administration as to generate freedom from war under the law of cause and effect? A study of her history suggests an affirmative answer. True, universal military service enables Switzerland to enforce respect for her neutrality, but on the other hand she has performed many internally and internationally beneficent actions. Matters concerning the welfare of the whole State are, for example, referred to the votes of all the citizens in a referendum. Switzerland was the first European country to adopt and practise the ideal of democracy. Since 1499 Swiss citizens have been able to breathe freely and discuss questionable matters without fear. Local government is carried on by democratic methods, and in elementary education

Switzerland ranks in advance of the rest of Europe. She has successfully solved the problem of welding three diverse Races—German, French and Italian—into one confederacy, united and working peaceably for the good of the country as a whole. Such enlightened internal rule and conduct could, I suggest, be properly regarded as sufficient, under the operation of the law of cause and effect, to keep a country free from war.

Switzerland a Benefactor of Mankind

This wise national direction is not all, however. Far from it. As a neutral State, Switzerland has been the seat of International Congresses of the greatest benefit to mankind as a whole. One of the earliest of these was concerned with the treatment of the wounded in war. This Congress was held in 1864 and from it there followed great amelioration of the suffering of war victims. The International Postal Congress was held in Berne in 1875. In consequence, almost all Nations agreed to carry each other's mail, thus drawing the peoples of the world into a closer relationship with each other. The League of Nations had its headquarters at Geneva and that most valuable of secular institutions, the International Red Cross, is also directed from this City. Is there not at least a poetic justice in this sequence of beneficent internal national life, combined with actions, bringing blessings to the whole of mankind on the one hand and, on the other, immunity from war to the country responsible for these good deeds?

Britain and the Commonwealth of Nations

Let us now consider Britain. She was involved in both World Wars, in which she suffered heavy losses of men and materials, yet she was not invaded and she emerged from both wars a victorious Nation. Evidently there have been both helpful and adverse activities in the past, each of which have contributed to the mixed *karma* of the British Nation.

Unfortunately, Britain's national history is not without its darker pages. England was long the centre of the feudal system. The conduct of the rich and the powerful during the rise of the industrial era left a great deal to be desired. As a colonising power some abuses were almost inevitable and, indeed, actually occurred. One grave error, amongst others, could have contributed to Britain's adversity. It was the Slave Trade in the new Colonies in North America in the reign of Charles II. When the second Virginia Company was founded in 1606 and tobacco was introduced, negro slaves were employed. The Southern Colonies and the tropical West Indian Islands needed man-power to work sugar, tobacco and rice plantations. Thus the Royal African Company was founded in 1671, in order to ensure a plentiful supply of slaves. The appalling extent of the trade may be gauged when we realise that by 1750 two hundred and fifty " slavers ", or slave ships, hailed from the Port of Liverpool alone.

Support for this reading of history in the light of the law of cause and effect is further supplied by the subsequent difficulties experienced in the United States in harmoniously weaving the thirteen million negro descendants of these slaves into the fabric of American social life. Racial cleavage, colour riots and lynchings, for example, constitute an unsolved problem, the causative origin of which lies far back in the days of the slave trade. England later found her conscience and abolished this trade, with compensation to the slave owners. This great act of national righteousness may be presumed to have modified the *karmic* effects of the practice of slavery and brought national advantages under the law of cause and effect.

A Sanctuary for the Oppressed

In addition, on the favourable side of Britain's account with Nature, as it were, we find also a colonisation which was not without its benefits to occupied countries, a generous treatment of the Boers after the South African War, the granting of freedom of religious worship to all her peoples and the introduction of the concept and practice of British law wherever her rule was established. Furthermore, Britain has always been a sanctuary, as has been discovered by the Jews, the Flemish weavers, the Hugenots after the massacre on St. Bartholomew's Eve, and by the French artistocrats during the French Revolution. More recently, the Basque children were brought and kept safe in Britain during the Civil War in Spain, as also were large numbers of refugees from Europe in both World Wars. Britain was a rallying ground from which the Monarchs, statesmen and military leaders and forces of the defeated European Nations found the help and the means to recover their national sovereignty. The Statute of Westminster gave complete freedom of the Dominions, and both wars were first entered upon on behalf of small Nations. Thus, if the idea of a principle of cause and effect is applied to British history, a peculiar appropriateness and exactness is discovered in the mixture of suffering and success which has characterised her more recent history.

Cruelty and Enslavement as Causes of Sorrow

If the views which I have been putting forward are at all acceptable and if, as I believe, they are indeed founded upon fact, then the great discovery has been made of the two root causes of human pain and sorrow, individual and national. Evidently these causes are cruelty and enslavement, including oppression and domination, whether mental, physical or both. Cruelty especially, of man to man, to children, to the aged and to the sick, as also to criminals—man's inhumanity to man—this produces a reaction in kind, is a cause which gives rise to an appropriate effect. If cruelty and enslavement generate suffering then, under *karmic* law, kindness and the giving of freedom must bring happiness.

Thus, history can provide us with a dual religious ideal: obedience to Divine law and unfailing kindness in national and individual conduct. A cynic has said that the message of history is that no one learns the message of history. Whilst admitting that, unfortunately, there is truth in this statement, I suggest that the central lesson of history, especially that of the immeasurable and long-continued suffering of mankind, when read in the light of the compensatory law, is: "I AM MY BROTHER'S KEEPER."

Harmlessness a Secret of Happiness

When applied directly to human conduct, day by day and hour by hour, the gospel of kindness could solve the world problems of war and the threat of war, and the individual problems of unhappiness and pain. To be kind is to ensure for oneself enduring happiness and peace. To be cruel is to make both of these pleasures quite unattainable. This gospel has been beautifully expressed in words pregnant with significance, despite their seeming simplicity: "Always be kinder than the situation demands."

PART FOUR

MAN'S EVOLUTION THROUGH SEVEN RACES ON EARTH

CHAPTER I

THE FINDINGS OF PHYSICAL AND OCCULT SCIENCE CONCERNING ATLANTIS AND THE ATLANTEANS

Atlantis—Fact or Fable?

Does the persistence of a legend throughout many centuries indicate a foundation of fact? How is it that similar monuments, cultural developments, flora, fauna and insects are found on both sides of the Atlantic? Was there once a land bridge? These are problems which nowadays are occupying many thoughtful minds.

Ancient Egypt Speaks

Soundings and explorations of the bed of the Atlantic Ocean, and recent expeditions in search of facts supporting the existence of Atlantis, have drawn public attention to the idea that such a continent may once have existed.

Apart from references in the Hindu *Puranas*, it was Plato who first related publicly the story of the people of Atlantis. He said that they formed the oldest civilisation in the world, possessed great cities with palaces, temples of gold with huge golden images of their deities, roads of great size and length and chains of canals, and rejoiced in a climate so benign that they reaped two harvests a year. They owned ships and war chariots, and bred the finest horses and cattle. Atlantis, said Plato, was situated in front of the Straits (of Gibraltar), then called the Pillars of Hercules, and led to a succession of Islands through which one might pass to the whole of the opposite continent, that is to say, to what is now America.

How did Plato hear all this? From his grandfather, Solon. During a visit to Egypt, Solon, the famous Athenian philosopher and lawgiver, was told of Atlantis by an aged priest at Sais, who added: "There dwelt in Atlantis the fairest and noblest race of men who ever lived, of whom you and your city are but a seed or remnant." The original Atlantis, he said, was pre-eminent in laws and possessed the finest constitution, whilst its citizens performed the noblest deeds; its antiquity was such that it was founded "by the goddess Athene a thousand years before Sais". It was "a great and wonderful empire, which had rule over the whole Island and several others, as well as over parts of the continent. A mighty power invaded it and also endeavoured to subdue our country (Egypt) and yours (Athens) and the whole land within the Straits (of Gibraltar). But violent earthquakes and floods in a single day and night caused the Island and its warlike men to sink beneath the seas." Such, in brief, is the ancient legend repeated by Plato. A vast continent existed which suffered invasion by a mighty host, a great war, and ultimate submersion through violent earthquakes and floods.

Justification for belief that such a great continent did once exist, linking the Americas with Africa and Europe, rests on quite a number of physical facts. Here are a few of them.

Scientific Evidence for Atlantis

The Dolphin Ridge, a plateau 9,000 feet above the Atlantic Ocean bed, extends from near the coast of Ireland to the coast line of South America, near French Guiana. Dry land fossils have been found on the bed of the Atlantic. Lava from this plateau, brought up by cable-laying vessels, is demonstrably dry land lava erupted less than 15,000 years ago. Mayan literature contains flood and creation stories clearly resembling those of *Genesis*, Egypt, India, Babylon and Chaldea.

Egyptian manuscripts located by Dr. Henry Schliemann, discoverer of Troy, have convinced him that Atlantis existed. One such manuscript records that an expedition was sent by Pharaoh about 7,650 B.C. to seek traces of the Motherland from whence Egyptians first came. None were found, however. Indeed, all had disappeared in the flood of 10,000 B.C. Nevertheless, it is a fact that Egyptian civilisation has no known root and no primitive period. A papyrus found by Dr. Schliemann, written by the priest-historian, Manetho, makes reference to a period 13,900 years ago as the date of the Kings of Atlantis in Egypt. Dr. Schliemann is said to have found at Troy an " owl vase" bearing Phoenician hieroglyphics reading: "From King Chronos of Atlantis." This peculiar owl vase was duplicated in a collection of objects from Tiahuenaco, South America.

Similarities of Architecture

Then, again, pyramids, monoliths and semicircles of stones like the Druid formations in England were found on the Island of Bonaco, off South America. Furthermore, the step pyramids of Egypt are duplicated in America. In American Indian languages there are over one hundred words that are similar to words of the same meaning in the Arabic and Greek languages. The myths of Greece, as, for example, that of Atlas, are repeated in Indian and Mayan tradition. In fact, the people of Atlantis were called A-T-L-S, and the syllable "Atl" is the root of many place names in America today, *e.g.*, Atlanta, Popocatepetl, and the name of the Toltec ruler and lawgiver, QUEXAL-CO-ATL.

Fauna and Flora

A close correspondence exists between the flora and fauna of the Southern U. S. A. and that of Europe. The monk seal does not frequent the open ocean, yet it is to be found in both the Mediterranean and the West Indies. Certain identical ants are found in the Azores and U. S. A. Moths and butterflies of the Canary Islands are identical with those in America, but none of these could fly across the Atlantic. The Basque language has no affinity with other European languages; it is, however, similar to aboriginal tongues of America in grammatical structure. Cro-Magnon skulls found in France resemble those found in Logoa Santa in Brazil. I think you will agree that these similarities cannot all be coincidences; there must once have been a land connection to account for them.

The Four Great Floods

What has Theosophy, whose teachings are the fruits of the occult investigations of countless generations of initiated seers, to say about Atlantis and the Atlanteans? A great deal, as reference to Theosophical literature will demonstrate. The history of Atlantis is said to be divided into four epochs, separated by four cataclysms. Up to 850,000 years ago, when a great flood occurred, Atlantis extended from a few degrees east of Iceland to about the site now occupied by Rio de Janeiro. It embraced Texas, the Gulf of Mexico, the southern and eastern States of America, Labrador and the area from there to Ireland, Scotland and a small portion of the North of England. It reached also from Brazil to the African Gold Coast.

The distribution of the land after the first great catastrophe of about 850,000 years ago, in the Pliocene Age, shows that a considerable portion of the north of the continent was submerged and the rest was much rent. The growing American continent was separated by a chasm from the remainder of Atlantis, which then occupied the bulk of the

Atlantic basin from about 50° N. latitude to a few degrees south of the Equator.

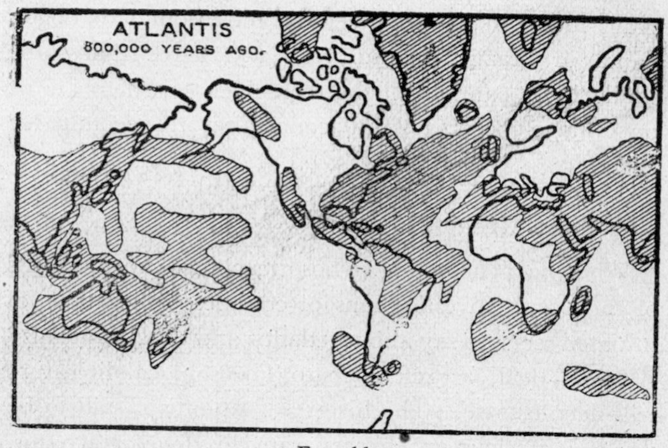

FIG. 1[1]

Great subsidences and upheavals also took place in other parts of the world. The British Isles, for example, then formed part of a huge Island embracing the Scandinavian Peninsula, the North of France and all the intervening and some of the surrounding seas.

The land surface, after the second catastrophe about 200,000 years ago, was much changed, although this cataclysm was relatively smaller than the first one. Atlantis proper was now split into a Northern Island called Ruta [2] and a Southern Island called Daitya [2]. The future North and South Americas were separated

[1] *Vide First Principles of Theosophy*, C. Jinarajadasa, The Theosophical Publishing House, Adyar, Madras, India.

[2] Ruta, Daitya: Sanskrit names in the Hindu Scriptures.

from one another. Egypt was submerged and the Scandinavian Island, which included the British Isles, was then joined to the future Europe.

FIG. 2

A stupendous planetary convulsion—the third of the four cataclysms—took place in 75,025 B.C. As a result Daitya, the Southern Island, almost entirely disappeared and Ruta was reduced to the comparatively small Island of Poseidonis, which was situated at about the centre of the Atlantic Ocean. The other land surfaces were then roughly as they are today, though the British Isles were still joined to Europe, the Baltic Sea was non-existent and the Sahara Desert was ocean.

In the fourth and final cataclysm of 10,000 years ago Poseidonis entirely disappeared, and its submergence brought up the Sahara Desert out of the sea and caused huge tidal waves in the Mediterranean countries. This is the historical basis for the story of the Deluge in the Bible and other ancient books.

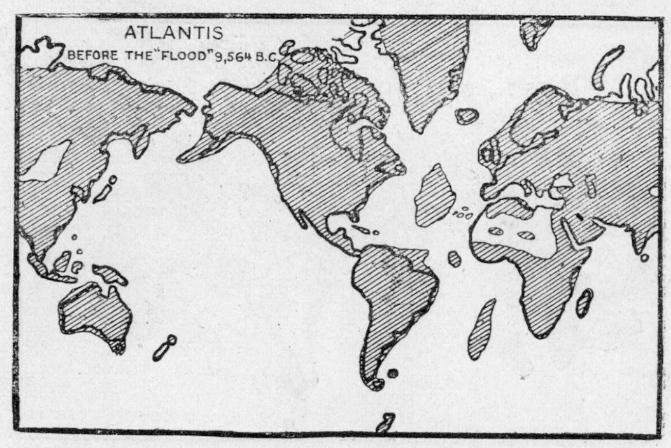

Fig. 3

The People of Atlantis

Theosophical teaching concerning the civilisation and people of Atlantis agrees with the descriptions given by Plato and also includes much additional information.[1] The Atlantean Race was the fourth of the seven major Races of men which will occupy this planet during the present World Period, itself the fourth in a series of seven. The fifth, or Aryan Race, is now in process of development. Naturally, great diversity of religion, politics and social structure was displayed throughout the long period of Atlantean development. Occult records exist of a very high

[1] *Vide The Solar System*, A. E. Powell, T. P. H., London.

state of culture achieved about the midpoint of the Atlantean Race and centred around the capital city—the famous City of the Golden Gates. This epoch is sometimes called the Toltec Golden Age; for an almost perfect communal society then existed for some 100,000 years. This civilisation was based upon the central idea: "From each according to his capacity, to each according to his need." During that time there was practically no crime and the most serious punishment consisted of banishment, which was dreaded.

Ancient Empire Builders

The Atlanteans were great colonisers, sailors and merchants. They founded an empire in Peru, and earlier still in Egypt. Eventually serious malpractises, including very evil forms of sorcery, developed and threatened the progress of the whole Atlantean Race. They recovered, however, and gave birth to the Aryan Race, for humanity ever progresses from Race to Race. The Atlanteans are, however, still numerically preponderant on the earth. Here is a list of some of the Nations which belong to that Race: the Laplanders, the Patagonians, the American Indians of both North and South Americas, the inland Chinese, the Basque people of Spain, the Magyars of Hungary, the Japanese and all the Monogolian, the Malayan and the Eskimo peoples.

Inspired with this knowledge, the Theosophist cannot despair, cannot fear that all human achievement could be swallowed up in unheeding, everlasting night. He knows that mankind moves through innumerable ages to ever-increasing power and wisdom and glory. *In hoc fide vivit et laborat.*[1]

* * * * *

Modern Testimony

Since this broadcast was delivered, the following apparent confirmation of Plato's report has appeared in the Press:

PASTOR FINDS ATLANTIS BY MEANS OF PLATO

" A German pastor, the Rev. Juergen Spanuth, claims that an expedition that he organised has found the king's castle and the temple of the fabled city of Atlantis in the North Sea, says the Associated Press correspondent in Hamburg.

" Herr Spanuth set out last month in a tiny boat for an area south of Heligoland to a spot which, he said, was closely described by Plato 2,000 years ago.

" He added ' We were deeply moved at the exactness of Plato's report. It was so exact that we sailed to the indicated spot, cast anchor five sea miles south of Heligoland, and after 10 minutes the diver reported he was standing on a man-made wall. When he measured that wall's width—30 metres—Plato's report was again confirmed. . . . The wall we found was about 6 ft. to 8 ft. high, and was traced over a distance of 900 yards.

[1] In this belief he lives and labours.

" 'The wall apparently once encircled the kingdom. Other smaller walls about 10 ft. wide must have belonged to the temple and royal castle. The ruins cover at least 60 acres on the sea floor.'

" Herr Spanuth, who has been searching for Atlantis for years, said he would fit out a new expedition and return with special diving equipment and dredges. The area was covered with deep sand, and therefore exploring could be successful only with the aid of expensive specially-built equipment."

The New Zealand Herald, 27-8-1952.

CHAPTER II

A NEW RACE AND A NEW AGE NOW BEING BORN

The Future of Man

HAS mankind reached the peak of its possible development in modern leaders of men? Is the human Race evolving, improving and unfolding greater powers? Will the present civilisation decline and fall, as its predecessors have done? These are vital problems. Theosophy makes a valuable contribution towards their solution.

The Cost of War

In the lifetime of most of us humanity has lived through years of the most diabolical evil the world has ever known. Estimates of the extent of the sufferings of mankind in the recent years of the Second World War are now available. The latest figures tell that forty-two and one half million people have died prematurely in these ten years. Nearly twenty-five million were civilian and seventeen and one half million were military deaths. These forty-two and one half million were men, women and children who were starved, tortured, shot, blown to bits, vivisected, frozen and gassed to death. They were deliberately murdered by every conceivable method of fiendish cruelty at the hands of supposedly civilised, cultured and mostly Christian Nations.

Since the end of the Second World War the Nations have sought unsuccessfully for that international unity and solidarity for which the great majority are longing. Thus far humanity seeks in vain to satisfy its growing hunger for wholeness, its longing for friendship, peace and security. Like twin swords of Damocles, atomic and bacteriological warfare hang over every Race, city and home on earth. In the face of these tragic facts man might well despair, not only of world peace in our time but of the whole future of the Race.

The Evolutionary Plan

What has Theosophy to offer to mankind at this juncture and in this hour of urgent need? The answer is *guiding principles*, knowledge of which is all-important, especially for those who aspire to play an effective part in the present world crisis. Theosophy provides that knowledge, for its study mentally lifts one to great heights from which a panoramic view of human life is possible. Theosophy reveals the master plan, one part of which concerns the evolution of the human Race. The total number of major Races is said to be seven, each of which is composed of seven successive sub-races. Five major Races have already appeared on earth, the Aryan peoples belonging to the fifth. Two Root Races lie in the future. Five sub-races of the fifth, the Aryan Race, have already appeared and a sixth is now being born. From this Theosophical teaching we learn that, being in the fifth of the seven Root Races, we are rather more than half way through our planet's life.

When considering racial evolution upon earth, it should be remembered that the same spiritual individuals, the same human Egos, incarnate in the successive Races. The Atlanteans, the Egyptians and the other ancient peoples were none other than ourselves. Similarly the members of the sixth sub-race and the sixth and seventh Root Races will only be new reincarnations of the same family of Egos, ourselves, for whom this earth has been appointed as the evolutionary field.

Birthplaces of a New Race

What, then, is the place of Australia [1] in this great plan, and what is the destiny of its peoples? Simply put, the answer is that the fifth Race is at this time giving birth to a sixth sub-race, and the countries of North America and Canada, South Africa, Australia and New Zealand are the chief places of its emergence. The sixth sub-race of the mother Aryan stock is coming into existence as a result of the emigration of European peoples, chiefly British, to the new racial homes. Even now the plan is well advanced. Each of these countries is already producing its typical variant of the new type. Indeed, the two World Wars may be regarded as both

[1] This Talk was broadcast in Australia.

the death throes of an old dispensation and the birth pangs of a new.

The Coming Race

What will the New Age man look like? Here is the young man. In Australia he is tall, wiry and somewhat slender of form. In New Zealand the build has perhaps been somewhat shorter and stockier up to now, though an increase in height is said to be occurring. The facial features of the sixth sub-race man, when they do show, are everywhere much the same. They are finely modelled, the nose tends to be long, the chin pointed and the forehead broad, thus making the face somewhat triangular. A certain eagerness, a vivid alertness, is stamped upon the whole countenance.

The women will especially display the quality of grace. They, too, will be slender and athletic, and the ideals of physical beauty and perfection will make great appeal to them. Again, the face will be triangular, the head pear-shaped, the features becoming clear-cut, regular and more and more refined as the new racial type is established. The texture of the skin will be notably fine and the hands and feet beautifully formed. So much for apparent physical trends.

What of the outlook? This also must be considered for, from the point of view of recent world events and the grave danger of a Third World War, the attitude of mind and the outlook of the new racial type are all-important. Can we forecast them? Yes, I think we can. The new psychological characteristics may be discerned by a study of advanced people throughout the world; for this new Race is not to be born in a single place, nor to belong to a single Nation. It is the type of the new humanity, which will seek unity and co-operation between free individuals and Nations. The very essence of all action in the sixth sub-race will be the union of many to achieve a single object, and not the dominance of one who compels others to his will. To advance together in freedom to a goal that all realise as desirable will ultimately become the method of attainment. This tendency to unity of action is one of the signs of racial evolution out of dependence upon mental processes, analysis, deduction and logic into the use of direct, intuitive perception.

Mankind's Will to World Unity

Despite grave difficulties at present appearing, signs are not wanting that this development is actually occurring. Indeed, it is abundantly evident today, for amid the welter of conflicting peoples and ideologies now evident, there is distinctly discernible a subtle yet powerful change taking place in the outlook of mankind upon the planet—the growth of one dominating idea with tremendous possibilities for the future. This change has been described as "a hunger for wholeness", and it is indeed a revolutionary event. It is almost comparable to a geological cataclysm, like the tilting of the earth's axis or a descent of an ice cap. It must culminate, I suggest, in an irresistible will to world unity.

This recognition of unity and determination to achieve it, characteristic of New Age man, will not only be physical and racial but mental and spiritual as well. Also, it will not only be local, but world-wide. Even now, this unifying tendency is discernible in the world and constitutes a definite sign of the emergence of the sixth sub-race of the fifth, the Aryan Race.

If one is looking for signs that any particular person is beginning to show the marks of that sixth sub-race today, such signs may be found in a growing intuitiveness and in a capacity to lead by love, sympathy and comprehension rather than by the dominance of an imperious will; for to advanced humanity dominance is anathema, freedom is a veritable religion. A synthesising spirit will be found in the forerunners of the sixth sub-race. They will be able to encourage and to unite diversity of opinion and of character, to gather round them the most unlike elements and to blend them, whilst still free, into a common whole.

Man Called to Collaborate in the Transcendental Task

Those who at present possess the capacity for taking into themselves diversities and sending them out again as unities, and for utilising widely varying individualities, finding each its place in freedom and welding all together into a strong whole—such people already display New Race characteristics. The ideal, as will be seen, is not a universalised set of conditions and a uniformity of human personality, but full individual development with readiness to combine and to co-operate in the great Causes of human happiness and progress.

Theosophy adds to the statement of this far-reaching plan the teaching that every individual can participate in the progress of the Race. Each one of us is important, for each of us can either help or hinder the historical process. If individually we will play a constructive part, if we can inspire our young people with the vision of themselves as Nation builders, then America, Canada, South Africa, Australia and New Zealand will fulfil their present promise of rapid advance to magnificent nationhood.

In the light of such teachings of Theosophy, the truly alarming portents to which I drew attention at the beginning of this Talk assume a less menacing aspect, dangerous though they are. The student of Theosophy need not fear that any futility overshadows man's highest dreams; he need not be afraid that civilisation will be swallowed up in unheeding, everlasting night; for he is taught that man moves through innumerable ages to ever-increasing power, wisdom and glory.

CHAPTER III

THE CHILDREN OF TODAY ARE THE CITIZENS OF TOMORROW

The Influence of Education

THE problem which I am now going to discuss is that of good citizenship and bad citizenship, particularly in the young people of today. Reports and statistics emanating from many countries and sources demonstrate that all is not as it should be with modern youth.

"Poets are born, not made", it is said, but good citizens are made, not born, and the same is true of bad citizens. Moral laxity in youth is largely the result of deficient education at home and at school, and of pernicious influences out in the world. In consequence, idealists are visualising an educational system with the main objectives of developing human character and of producing good citizens of the home, the school, the city, the Nation and the World. Advanced thinkers have long been proclaiming the urgent need for education for character-building, stability and integrity. They seek to imbue young people with a strong moral sense and a vision of excellence. Education for successful living and for useful citizenship, including public service, is now being regarded as both the key to the New World Order and the life blood of civilisation.

Education is of two parts—in school and out of school. At present these two influences upon the growing child tend to become divorced. Teachers state that the good they try to do in the school is all too often undone at home and out in the world. In-school and out-of-school education should be co-ordinated, otherwise the one nullifies the other. The home will then widen naturally into the school, which in its turn becomes both an extension of the home and a natural gateway to adult life.

Moral Dangers

The grave dangers confronting youth after leaving school arise from contact with adult materialism, selfishness, commercialism and vice. Girls and boys go out into life without the necessary guidance and protection against moral danger and insufficiently supported by belief in spiritual and moral principles. In consequence, they are often helpless in the presence of the evils and tendencies to evil which surround them in the world.

Radio and Cinema

Broadcasting is one example of these dangers. The radio penetrates nearly every home. The majority of children are exposed to it from babyhood. Sensational stories, luring advertisements, moronic crooning and raucous jazz pour out of loudspeakers throughout the Nations. Due censorship, with the single purpose of producing good citizens, is urgently needed to combat this very serious evil.[1]

Advertising may be taken as another example. The newspapers, the hoardings, the handbills and some of the radio stations of the world are designed for advertising. This almost hypnotic procedure beats upon the consciousness of modern man, influencing thought and word and deed. The adult gradually acquires a self-defence against this perpetual battering. Unfortunately that defence is cynicism. The child, however, does not know any better and is inevitably affected, deceived, moulded. The predominant motive of commercial advertising is to get, to acquire, to deceive, to persuade, to allure one's fellow men. It is selfish, acquisitive. The child tends to conclude that cleverness in deceit for personal profit wins the world's greatest prizes. He absorbs this attitude towards life, gravely to his detriment, thinking of success in purely worldly terms and material values.

Many children are thus spoilt, marred as potential good citizens. They are sent out into life with a strong desire to advertise themselves, to sell themselves, their education, their scholastic degrees, their highest gifts, for money, power, possessions. Thus the young people of today are being moulded by adults into selfish embodiments of a ravenous passion for getting things. Of religion, of the Divine Presence, they know naught.

[1] This passage was omitted when broadcasting.

Their minds are not spiritually moulded. A modern child's grace is reported to have been: "This food comes to us by courtesy of God Almighty." A story is told of another child who, when shown by her mother her first rainbow, immediately asked: "What is it supposed to advertise?"

Undue Acquisitiveness

Excuse me if I seem to over-stress this commercial element. It is, I think, the key to the present deplorable situation. The child, as soon as he is old enough, perceives humanity perpetually advertising itself and its wares, luring, deceiving, setting baits to entrap the unwary. He receives an education which is predominantly materialistic, in which true religion has only a minor part. The child is taught to memorise facts and ideas in order that, by repeating them correctly at examinations, he will win educational rewards, defeat his fellow pupils and shine over them, and then sell the whole result of education in the market place. Doubtless it was this perversion of the true purpose of education—which is, I suggest, to draw out inherent faculties rather than only to drive in ideas from without—that caused Mark Twain to say: "Education is not so swift as massacre, but it is far more deadly in the long run."

All this combative, competitive, acquisitive, materialistic education is a crime against the child. It is, therefore, a crime against adults and so a crime against humanity. Excessive commercialisation is, I conclude, the greatest single external cause of the unhappiness of man amidst an excess of this world's goods.

The child has no chance against all this. Unless an advanced Ego and especially fortunate in parents, teachers, companions and employers, he grows up like his surroundings and his fellow men. His character reflects his environment. *With numerous individual exceptions*, he becomes moulded by both into a self-centred, acquisitive animal, bereft of either spirituality or culture. If to this be added the outbreak and the nature of the two World Wars and the threat of a third, is it small wonder that so many young people (*far from all*) grow up into selfish, self-indulgent and materially minded cynics.

Sex Education

There is also the other pressing problem of guidance in the exercise of the creative functions of the body. How, where and by whom should this guidance be given? Let me suggest an answer. As soon as they are old enough, that is as soon as they notice the difference of sex and begin to enquire, young people should be wisely given adequate knowledge of the creative functions of their bodies. They should not grow up in ignorance either of the place and purpose of sex in human life or of the grievous effects of its misuse. Especially should they be unmistakably aware of the dangers of sexual indulgence to both body and soul.

How should this guidance be given? It should at first, I submit, be a highly individual and very private instruction, received preferably from one whom the boy or girl loves and trusts. Ideally, I conclude, mothers should guide girls and fathers instruct boys. Primarily this is the responsibility of the parents and of no one else. The wise and sympathetic family doctor or the enlightened minister may, however, assist or even replace the parents should they not feel equal to the task. The right occasions and the right presentation are of supreme importance and the truth must be told, not untruths. In the absence of State clinics founded for the purpose, as in the New Age we hope they will be, and in the absence of experts trained for the task, parents can and do make or mar their children by their own example and by their fulfilment or neglect of parental responsibility in this most important matter. Thus I submit that a home with a strong moral atmosphere based upon Christlike love is a form of instruction and guidance for life for which there is no alternative.

Civilisation Marches Forward on the Feet of Little Children

The importance of especial care of the youth of the Nation cannot, I suggest, be over-estimated. Civilisation marches forward on the feet of little children. The post-war world must be a world characterised especially by great advances in education. The New Age must be the age of the child and the freedom-loving Nations will do well to direct their immense resources to the spiritual, the moral and the physical welfare of the youth of the world, by whom the New Age must be built. This would involve a world-wide extension of educational facilities for young and old, first and foremost to save mankind from threatened annihilation by atomic weapons and second to produce the finest possible types of human beings, and so of human civilisation.

CHAPTER IV

INSPIRED LEADERS—HOW THEY MAY BE FOUND AND TRAINED

Humanity Astray

WHAT is the greatest need of the world today? I suppose we might all answer differently. Let me offer an idea. In the critical times through which humanity has passed during the first half of the Twentieth Century it must, I think, be admitted that the great need of mankind today is for inspired leadership. Humanity needs men and women to whom it can give complete and wholehearted respect because of their fine attainments, spiritually, intellectually and culturally, and the splendid human beings they are. Winston Churchill proved to be just such a leader during the Second World War. He aroused, inspired, encouraged and led the British people through their darkest time, which he called " their finest hour ". In consequence of Churchill's leadership those times of trial did, in fact, become their finest, greatest hours. We should remember, however, that peace, no less than war, also demands leadership.

The urgent necessities of war, the pressing threats of invasion, death and enslavement, though not entirely banished, are not immediately overshadowing the peoples of the world's democracies. Numerous and far-reaching dangers do, however, still threaten mankind. We are under attack both from within, in the moral sense, and from without as a result of subversive influences and the threat of the outbreak of a third aggressive war. To guide us through these dangers, leaders can prove extremely valuable. Great men and women, alive to the hazards of our times, are amongst us but there are not enough of them. It seems as if the dead weight of apathy, the corroding influence of cynicism, the deliberate undermining of the stability of the Democratic States, and the continued excitation to over-indulgences as in sex, alcohol, drugs and gambling, almost nullify the efforts of the all-too-few spiritual and cultural leaders of the modern world. Therefore, the need for more great men and women in the world is urgent.

The Call for Guidance

Is there any hope for the emergence of leaders? More important, can we ourselves do anything to prepare the way for the birth amongst us of truly great Souls or, as we say Theosophically, advanced Egos? If reincarnation be true, can the rebirth of great leaders from the past be hoped for and, if so, what are the conditions which prospective parents should provide? Let me suggest an answer. It is generally agreed that a new and higher type of human being is now appearing in the world. In consequence, there is hope that a new civilisation, a new World Order and a new (re-expressed) World Religion will be established on earth. Obviously we are on the threshold of great changes, are at the dawn of a new day in the life of our planet.

By what processes will such advanced men and women come into existence and the new dispensation displace the old? More important still, what can be done to prepare the way for them? The essentials appear to be at least two-fold. First, the incarnation of advanced Egos and second, the provision of suitable environment and education, these two being to a considerable extent mutually interdependent. Advanced Egos require both special kinds of bodies and special opportunities for the fulfilment of their mission as world leaders. From this it would appear that the parents and the teachers of today are favoured with unique opportunities.

Parental Opportunities

What, then, may we assume, is the parenta contribution to the birth of the special types of bodies into which advanced Souls may incarnate? First, it is probable that such parents would have a wide and catholic outlook on life. Their interests would extend far beyond the round of domestic, recreational, business, or professional life. Where circumstances permit, they would be actively concerned with interests larger than those of their own immediate preoccupations. Such great Causes as Child Welfare Movements, civic, state and national affairs and, particularly in these days the United Nations Organisation, would be likely to attract them. New Age[1] parents would naturally have great appreciation of beauty and in many cases be proficient in one of the Arts. The love of beauty would be an outstanding characteristic of their natures and would show itself in their homes and the lives they live.

The Religion of the Future

What would be likely to be the religious views of such forward-looking people? Their religion would probably be both mystical and practical. Some form of devotional exercise leading to individual experience of union with God would doubtless be employed, thus also keeping open the channels between the Inner, Immortal Self and the personal, bodily life and consciousness. Extremes of belief and practice, and constant changes of philosophic and religious attachment, would naturally be avoided. So much for the probable and desirable parental ideals. What may we suppose are the more material essentials, especially for the attraction into a family of advanced Souls?

The Adverse Effects of Alcohol

At this point I wish to dissociate myself from the Theosophical Society and to express a purely personal opinion about pre-natal necessities for the production of first-class physical bodies and brains. After some forty

[1] For the sense in which this term is used see Chapter II, Part Four, p. 100.

years' study of social problems and of practical work in various Reform Movements, I have been forced to the conclusion that abstinence from alcohol is essential in those parents who would give birth to the finest types of children. Alcohol and drugs can bedull the brain and nervous system and, in consequence, shut the Spiritual Self out of the individual's life particularly as far as intuition and other spiritualising impulses are concerned. I know that I am presenting ideals which may sound extreme, but the world need is so great at this time that it is worth our while to consider high ideals, especially concerning marriage, parenthood and child training. Procreation and childbirth, for instance, should be recognised as divine acts, Sacraments in very truth, since they are human enactments of the great and continuous process of creation [1] which is enacted by the one Divine Creator of all.

Preparations for Motherhood

The period of pre-natal life is of the utmost importance in the production of the finest type of body and the incarnation of the highest type of Ego. Throughout the whole period the home should be as harmonious as possible and everything should be done to keep the mother healthy and happy. So far as material responsibilities permit she, herself, should centre her thoughts upon ideals of beauty, peace and the service of the world.

[1] Not of something out of nothing, but rather emanation from a latent to an active state.

The Gift of Freedom

At this point a word of warning may be useful. Whilst all these external preparations for the child, if wisely made, can be productive of nothing but good, it should never be forgotten that no limitations should be put upon the child itself. No mental or emotional pressure to follow any particular line of thought, or parentally chosen, specific mode of life, should be applied to the incarnating Ego, whose freedom should at all times be most zealously guarded. Parents are rightly concerned with the mental, the emotional and the physical conditions during gestation, at birth and afterwards, but the interior life of the child, the Egoic intention, must ever be respected. This may then be fulfilled unhampered by external pressure. That restriction apart, the joy of attracting an advanced Ego and of producing a healthy and beautiful body is within reach of reasonably healthy, married people who care to provide the conditions to which I have referred.

Children of Today, the Leaders of Tomorrow

In conclusion, I repeat the conviction that the world suffers today from lack of wise and inspired leadership. Where, then, are the urgently needed leaders to be found and trained? Surely the answer is: "Amongst the children now being born and amongst the children now at school." Despite the pressing necessities inseparable from the maintenance of the routine of education, members of the educational profession especially should be on the look-out for leaders, should watch for the spark of genius in every child who comes to them and should do their utmost to fan it—and especially the latent talent for leadership—into a flame.

"Look out for leaders" might well be a guiding principle for both the educational profession and parents throughout the world. Thus may be found and trained great servants of the Race. Thus, in this period of dire need, there may be given to the world spiritual teachers, statesmen, educators, scientists and artists, who will carry humanity through the present dangers into the security and co-operation essential to the fulfilment of man's dream of world brotherhood and world peace.

CHAPTER V

EDUCATION FOR FINE CITIZENSHIP

The Child as a Person

How did ancient civilisations produce great men and women, literature, art and engineering achievements without the aid of modern education? What is " the mystery of a person "? (Carlyle.) Are " children born persons " or are they just girls and boys? Why did the Christ place so great a value upon " these little ones "? Should children be protected from the tyranny of the adult? Should a child be restricted at all points? Must we be like the mother in *Punch:* " Go and see what Tommy is doing and tell him he mustn't." ? Should children be brought up on " do " and " dont " ? Are intelligence and industry at school to be decided only by marks? Should corporal punishment be displaced by " the new discipline " ?

Repression or Redirection?

In offering a reply to the last of these vital questions I am expressing purely personal, rather than Theosophical, opinions concerning one great need of the world today. As I suggested in a previous Talk on this subject, one need is for spiritual, intellectual, cultural and political[1] leaders. I have already made suggestions concerning the influence of parental idealism and the conditions of pre-natal life upon the development of the child.

What are the fundamentals in the training of leaders, as indeed of all children? One is, I suggest, that the world outlook, the planetary vision[2] should be inculcated from the beginning. Another is that all discipline should take the form of a redirection rather than a suppression of the upwelling, and often overflowing, energies of youth.

Spare the Rod and Spoil the Child??

Sir Edmund Gosse, in his enjoyable book, *Father and Son: A Study in Temperaments*, tells of an incident which occurred when he was six years old. He had been guilty of disobedience and his father, after a solemn sermon, chastised him sacrificially by giving him several cuts with a cane. Sir Edmund Gosse writes: " I have to confess with shame that I went about the house for some days with a murderous hatred of my father locked within my bosom."

I am aware of the view that a good thrashing does no one any harm, but find myself quite unable to accept it. I know that whilst an immense change is taking place in the theory and practice of child training,

[1] Politics, the science of State organisation.

[2] This subject receives consideration in Chapter II, Part Four, p. 104.

as a result of which a spirit of individuality and co-operation pervades the modern class room, masters and mistresses of the old type still hammer their will upon the children in their care. Such teachers are generally themselves insensitive, unsympathetic and uninspired, whilst the children are all too often devitalised. They have been described as "plastic lumps to be crushed into a given mould", the result being "standardisation or illiteracy. . . . The cane was the sceptre, symbol of power in an age of mental and emotional torture. Mental torture, for those who were punished knew beforehand of the impending strokes, and the mental suspense was greater pain than the physical shock. Emotional torture, because all self-respect vanishes when one becomes a beaten unit in a fear-ridden group." School became "intermittent warfare. . . . The odds were on the teacher and all the losses against the child. . . . There was no redress except in cases of extreme brutality and this was, and is, always difficult to establish as fact." [1]

The effects of such a system, and especially of such punishments, make a lasting impression upon the developing adult. Shocks sustained by the child can become firmly embedded in the subconscious mind and remain as a hidden and potential adverse influence throughout the whole life. These problems resolve themselves into the queries: when to punish, when not to punish and how to punish?

[1] *The Psychology of Punishment*, Arthur B. Allen, L.C.P., F.R.S.A., A. Coll. H., Allman and Son Ltd., 73 Minories, London.

Corporal Punishment not a Remedy

Consideration of these questions brings me, with many modern educationalists and psychologists, to a strongly held personal conviction. It is that corporal punishment should be unthinkable, not only where new and more sensitive children are concerned, but in the training of all children. It not only does not remedy misconduct, but by the shock which it gives, both to body and *psyche*,[1] intensifies the existing causes of difficulty and in addition is most likely to create new ones; for what greater shock could there be to a child than the humiliation and pain of corporal punishment administered by those hitherto trusted and loved?

Right conduct is dependent upon a harmonious relationship between the Spiritual Soul or Inner Self of man, the mind, the emotions and the physical body; for these interact upon each other continually, conditions in one of them being reflected in all of the others. Every physical shock, for example, disturbs the harmonious relationship which normally exists throughout the whole nature of a healthy, happy child.[2] It then becomes difficult for the Ego, the Spiritual Self within, to express itself through, and control the actions of its new vehicles. One imagines that, when the time for rebirth approaches, Egoic prevision of the possibility of corporal punishment, either at home or at school, would cause the advanced Soul to choose a more favourable parentage and environment, if such were

[1] *Psyche* (*Gr.*), Mind or Soul.

[2] For a fuller exposition of this subject see Chapter I, Part Six.

within its *karma*; [1] for when a certain stage of development has been reached a considerable measure of freedom is granted to a reincarnating Ego in the choice of the Nation, the family and the conditions into which it will be reborn. Since the world's need for inspired leadership can only be met by the reincarnation of such highly developed human beings, it is important that no unnecessary obstacles should be put in the way of rebirth into an otherwise favourable environment. Nothing, one assumes, would drive a highly evolved, and therefore sensitive, individual away from prospective parents and teachers more than the existence in them of the disrespect and the streak of sadistic brutality from which the infliction of severe corporal punishment arises.

"Spare the Rod and Spoil the Child", an Erroneous Doctrine

Observation of children and adults, who have been brought up on the "spare the rod and spoil the child" principle, has shown that many of them have been spiritually and intellectually deadened, and psychically and physically coarsened, as a result of the frequent infliction of corporal punishment.[2]

In a broadcast, which was also printed in *The Broadcaster* of West Australia, February 23rd 1952,

[1] The law of cause and effect. See Chapter I, Part Three, p. 57.

[2] For a fuller exposition of this subject see *The Psychology of Punishment*, Arthur B. Allen, L.C.P., F.R.S.A., A. Coll. H., and *Children as "Persons"*, Charlotte M. Mason, Parents' National Educational Union, 28 Victoria Street, London.

Dr. Ruth Sheffield stated that: " Regulations made under the Education Act in this State impose strict limits on the use of corporal punishment in our schools. The limits are not always observed, it is reported, but the Education Department can and does invoke the regulations to deal with errant teachers reported by parents. The boxing of children's ears is strictly forbidden. So, too, is corporal punishment for girls aged twelve years and over. Corporal punishment for girls below the age of twelve is allowed only in very extreme circumstances. If it is to be inflicted it is to be carried out only by a female teacher. When corporal punishment is inflicted on girls, a statement of the circumstances and a full report must be sent to the district superintendent. Generally, corporal punishment may, as a last resort, be inflicted by the head teacher only and may be employed for offences against morality, gross impertinence or wilful and persistent disobedience. Corporal punishment shall not be inflicted for failure or inability to learn, for trivial breaches of school discipline or for neglect to prepare home lessons."

Bad Citizens are made, not Born

" Juvenile delinquents ", continues Dr. Sheffield, " get better treatment than our school children! This dawned on me when I learnt from a kindly Children's Court magistrate that ' corporal punishment is out of date now in our Children's Courts ', and further that ' nowadays there's help and sympathy, not a beating, for the youngster who goes too far.'

"This corporal punishment is no preparation for good citizenship! We don't want stunted, fearful or aggressive children who resent or distrust authority and cannot get along happily with their fellow men. But without more intelligent goodwill and wisdom in dealing with children, that is all we are going to reap. Let's face it. Beatings, strappings and other harsh punishments are autocratic measures, worthy only of the dictator state that needs to prove that 'might is right'. They are contrary to the fundamentals of democracy and the United Nations Charter, both of which proclaim the freedom and dignity of the individual, whatever his race, nationality—or age! It's time, therefore, that we, the parents of Australia, and trustees for the nation's future, unite in demanding the abolition of corporal punishment in our schools." Such is the expressed opinion of a medical specialist, Dr. Ruth Sheffield.

What is the alternative to smacking and thrashing? I suggest it is a wise, firm redirection of often unwittingly misdirected energies and interests and a continual appeal to reason.

Hypersensitivity and the Modern Child

This brings me to a rather strange phenomenon of our times. I refer to the growing evidence for the presence and activity of supernormal faculties. This has become so marked that the existence of what has come to be called Extra Sensory Perception in man has been demonstrated after extensive laboratory tests.[1] This hypersensitivity often shows itself quite early. Children display uncanny wisdom and unusual perception at times. Such young people require special care and this poses a difficult problem for parents and teachers. I suggest that when there are psychic powers, these should be treated as quite natural. They should not be either encouraged or discouraged; rather should they be taken for granted, so that the child may grow up to think of them as perfectly normal. On no occasion should they be made the subject of parade before others.

Parents and teachers should also remember that the psychic child is far more sensitive in every way than the non-psychic. Using always common sense, all treatment should be gentler, kinder and more lenient than is usually given to the robust, objective type of child; for the greater sensitivity produces more intense response to disciplinary correction, and especially to the mental aspects of any punishment which may be deemed necessary. Such children should never be corrected publicly on this account. When they have done wrong, their psychic nature causes them to experience an extreme sense of guilt and humiliation. They tend to brood unduly upon their error and upon any injustice in the treatment meted out to them. This may set up complexes which can later destroy health and happiness, especially since the psychic child is also subject to influences and forces to which non-psychic types are unresponsive. These inevitably affect his

[1] For fuller information on this subject see *The Reach of the Mind*, Dr. J. B. Rhine.

conduct and may lead him, if not protected, into errors into which the normal child would not fall.

The Importance of Environment and Training

All these considerations are of especial importance just now; for whilst it is true that the finest types of human beings, the leaders and geniuses of the New Age, will be advanced Egos, there would appear to be in addition very large numbers of children being born at this period who, under right training, could develop into wise leaders of men. This presupposes that, as Egos, they have the necessary development and evolutionary experience behind them. If they have and are born under helpful parental, climatic and magnetic conditions, then with the right education they could become powerful influences for good in their community. This is especially true at the present time; for whilst leaders with magnetic personalities generally arise in response to crises and special opportunities, personal and national, the present may justly be regarded as both intensely critical and full of opportunities for the display of those qualities which are the mark of the true leader.

A Leader of Men

What are the chief qualities to be developed in a would-be leader? [1] Some of them, I suggest, are: capacity for sublimated selfhood; the sense of a great

[1] For a full exposition of this subject, see *Leadership Through the Ages*, Lieut.-Gen. Sir George MacMunn, K.C.B., K.C.S.I., D.S.O., Alexander Maclehose & Co., 58 Bloomsbury St., London.

mission and of having the power to fulfil it; self-confidence; vision, ability and will to recognise and answer the call when it comes; courage, physical and mental; earnestness; integrity; knowledge of the world; faculty for handling men; camaraderie; enthusiasm and fervour; joy of living; sympathy; health; capacity to be inspired on occasion and to convey that sense of uplift to those who are to be led; knowledge of guiding principles; insight into first causes; humility; an inherent goodliness and godliness; a flair for propaganda; calmness on some occasions and fire on others; oratory.

When practicable the child should visit foreign countries, for the mental outlook of the leader-to-be must be broad, tolerant and co-operative—and more especially, I suggest, concerning non-Christian religions and peoples. The planetary view must continually be inculcated and the child taught to see humanity as a whole, and to realise the interdependence of man upon man and of Nation upon Nation.

Education Means "Drawing out"

In conclusion, it seems to me to be most important that both parents and teachers should have the right attitude to their parental and tutorial offices. They should, for example, be conscious of a profound respect for the Divine Self within every child. They should recognise the laws which govern man's evolutionary development, especially the laws of rebirth and cause and effect. In addition, I suggest, they should have the educative sense, which means they would ever be watching for revelations of the child's own innate qualities, natural power and inherent knowledge brought over from past lives. Perceiving these attributes, they should ever be ready to assist in their fullest and freest expression.

Briefly expressed, these, I believe, are the main principles upon which the treatment of all children should be founded. Were they applied, a very large percentage of modern children could be changed from ordinary to outstanding types, from mediocrity to genius, from followers to leaders and, I repeat, it is wise and inspired leaders who are so greatly needed in the world today.

PART FIVE

WORLD PEACE
AND OUR PERSONAL RESPONSIBILITY

CHAPTER I

MANKIND'S PROGRESS TOWARDS WORLD CO-OPERATION

War or Peace?

THE great questions which most of us are asking at this time surely are: What is ahead of us—the Third World War which seems to threaten, or the establishment of a stable peace? Which is it to be—world enslavement by a tyrannical power or world freedom? Must we go on indefinitely as we are at the time of writing, divided into two armed camps, or can humanity become united into one co-operative family of Nations?

Before I offer an answer, I wish to make it clear that for me the ideal of a united humanity means a free humanity living in harmonious relationship. I do not mean a totalitarian world—one united under a dictator. I do not mean unity brought about by domination, by force and by fear. I mean world co-operation by free peoples living under a democratic parliamentary system.

The Historical Process

Is such a functional unity of mankind too much to hope for? In answer, I am going to enunciate three fundamental ideals. First, that world peace will eventually arrive as a result of the development in the human mind of the power to perceive unity amidst diversity. When a sufficient number of people are able to recognise in the human Race a shared life and a common goal of spiritual excellence, then—and not until then—will lasting peace have become a possibility. The second idea is that the historical process, the evolutionary trend, is demonstrably in the direction of international co-operation. The third idea concerns the contribution which the individual can make towards world unification.

Concerning the first of these three ideas—the necessity for the intellectual perception of a shared life in all human beings—I do not believe that this is too much to hope for. There are indications that intense, competitive individualism is, very slowly, giving place to a recognition of the mutual interdependence of Nation upon Nation and of man upon man. True, the formal, analytical mind is naturally individualistic and competitive, but as the higher attributes of the human intellect develop the sense of self-separateness diminishes. The concepts of unity and of co-operation for the welfare of all then assume an increasing dominance. This growing recognition of unity will culminate in the ultimate establishment on earth of world co-operation founded upon the principles of brotherhood, justice and peace. The League of Nations, the United Nations Organisation and all the other Movements working for international co-operation are, I submit, outward signs of this mental development in man, which has been aptly described as " a hunger for wholeness ".

The International Spirit

This brings me to my second idea—the historical process or general evolutionary trend. Recent history, despite the tragedy of the two World Wars, indicates that there is factual support for guarded optimism. Here is a partial list, which could be greatly extended, of achievements of world unification and international co-operation during the last hundred years or so: The League of Nations; the United Nations Organisation and all its many specialised agencies, such as UNNRA, UNESCO, UNICEF (United Nations International Children's Emergency Fund); the United States of America; the British Commonwealth of Nations; the Pan-American Union; the Boy Scouts; the Girl Guides; the Y.M.C.A.; the Y.W.C.A.; Rotary, with its ideal of service above self; the International Red Cross; the International Postal Convention under which all Nations agree to carry each other's mail; the International . . . " Rules of the Road " and Code of Signals for use at sea and in the air; Greenwich Mean Time; the International system of units and symbols in science; the British pharmacopoeia and nomenclatures in anatomy, medicine and meteorology; International nomenclature in music; International Laws, *e.g.*, Patent and Copyright Laws, and the Olympic Games.

What have these achievements of unity in common? The answer, I suggest, is an international spirit, a planetary outlook, a vision of a global civilisation, a recognition of the unity and interdependence of Nation upon Nation and of man upon man. So we see from history that, despite inevitable divisions, mankind does display the power to rise above and think beyond purely national boundaries. Some members of the human Race, at any rate, are beginning to see the world as a whole. The evolutionary trend is obviously towards unification.

There is ground, therefore, for vigilant hope that the historical process will continue until modern man's increasing " hunger for wholeness " brings into existence a united humanity. In consequence of their longing for world friendship, the time is certain to come when the peoples of the earth will agree that human advancement in both spiritual excellence and physical welfare is the common goal of all mankind. Universal peace will then be seen as essential to the attainment of that goal. Justice, in its turn, will be recognised as the pre-requisite of peace, for peace and justice stand or fall together.

The Opportunity of the Individual

How soon can world unity be attained and must there be a third World War? These two questions press for answers. Quite clearly, the reply to both of them is: *that depends upon you and upon me*. What, then, can we do? This brings me to my third idea, the place of the individual in the present crisis. In order to discover that place, let us first look at the latest expression of the movement towards world unity—the United Nations.

The Ineffectiveness of U.N.O.

The chief British delegate to the United Nations, Sir Gladwyn Jebb, speaking in Ottawa on October the 8th, 1952, said that the racial problem could " wreck the whole concept of the United Nations. While industrialisation is being welcomed as having led to the raising of living standards it is suspected in under-developed countries as being in some way associated with European domination."

Sir Gladwyn continued: " These are the doubts and fears which so largely animate the so-called Arab-Asian group in the United Nations. This group is admittedly not held together by any common interest, but only by hatred of ' colonialism ' and consequent suspicion of the Western races as such. This attitude is dangerous as tending to stimulate race consciousness and race discrimination in vast areas. It is based on emotions that have become out of date. I feel that these class-conscious, race-conscious emotions are really one of the greatest dangers to the United Nations. . . "

Despite much fine humanitarian work in the alleviation of suffering, sickness and misery, U. N. has proved to be completely ineffectual when dealing with such grave situations as those of Korea, Indo-China, Malaya, Persia, Egypt and South Africa. What, may we presume, is the cause of this failure? I suggest that it is very largely due to a lack of support from the individual members of the component Nations.

This is both surprising and somewhat disheartening, for the advantages of closer co-operation between Governments in order to solve common problems and share discoveries and techniques for improving the lot of man are so obvious that they hardly need to be enumerated. The ideals of the United Nations must appeal to men and women of almost all national, religious and economic groups. These ideals cannot be translated into practical terms, however, unless the citizens of the component Nations give their fullest support to this supremely significant task. Special programmes in one's own country can be helped and local U. N. O.s supported. This collaboration by the individual will help greatly to solve the present problem of collective security, particularly in face of the threat of aggression. The great cost in men, money and material involved in military resistance to aggressor Nations causes Governments to hesitate before embarking upon such a costly procedure. The mounting casualties, financial drain and present indecisiveness of the Korean War, waged for just such a purpose, underscore this difficulty with which U. N. is faced in the fulfilment of that part of its task which concerns the establishment and maintenance of world peace.

The Importance of International Co-operation

In order that we as private citizens may comprehend the nature of our personal responsibilities, let us now follow the idea of international co-operation a little further. So far as organised world co-operation is concerned, a World Government which is able to solve conflicts between Nations by judicial decision is essential. Furthermore, the component National Governments must be ready to give to the World Power the sole disposition of offensive weapons; for a Nation can only be regarded as being sincerely peace-loving if it is ready to surrender its military forces to International authority and to renounce every attempt to achieve self-expansion by the use of force and even the means to do so. Law and order must be established in the field of international relations. Unfortunately, in the present individualistic, acquisitive and fiercely competitive phase of the development of the human mind, national instinct, feeling and ways of thought, rooted deep in habit and history, render the formation and successful operation of a World Government exceedingly difficult.

Power Politics

This is largely on account of what is known as power politics. Present-day international political philosophy throws much reliance on force, cunning and the *dicta*: " Let him take who has the power and let him keep who can " and " Since all right is founded in power, let us get power and none will dispute our right." Able political philosophers support this view, holding that honour, morality and goodwill are but useful myths, which must give way to force and cunning when real interests clash. The attitude and practice of power politics has long been that conscience is a jest, a mere engine of priestcraft. This is exemplified in the problems which beset the League of Nations and are now besetting U. N., the North Atlantic Treaty Organisation (N.A.T.O.) and the Council of Europe.

Nevertheless there is hope, for collective security is now firmly established between all the members of the British Commonwealth of Nations. This is the case in the Americas also for, in the Munro Doctrine, the U. S. A. has said in effect, "An attack on any American Republic is an attack upon us." Even so, the consent and the co-operation of the individuals who compose these Nations are essential; for the underlying principle of a successful unification of World States would be the fulfilment by everyone, everywhere, of the duty to serve with word and deed the spiritual and physical advancement of the whole human Race. This would be accepted by all generations of men as their common Cause. Man will then have learned to do unto others as he would like others to do unto him, and especially to abstain from violence except for the repulse of violence as commanded or granted under law. Acceptance and fulfilment by individuals and Nations of this their duty towards each other must be recognised as the heart and crux of the problems of world unity and world peace; for without this acceptance and fulfilment of duty by the majority of mankind, it is feared that U. N. will continue to be impotent in the face of the threat of war. Indeed, what we and our fellow men do or fail to do within the next few years can determine the fate of our civilisation.

The Hunger for Wholeness

Thus, the recognition and fulfilment of duty is the ideal. What, then, is the actuality? Apparently two main attitudes and standards exist. They are held by two classes of people—those who perceive the truth of unity and brotherhood and those who do not. Those who do are men and women who have come to know unity as if by instinct, or rather intuition. Such people perceive disunity as a denial of truth, and feel impelled to labour in order to reveal their vision to others and to promote world unity. They are responsible for the League of Nations, U.N., Rotary, Boy Scouts, Y.M.C.A., Y.W.C.A., the International Red Cross and the many other Movements based on brotherhood and service.

Happily, the number of men and women in whom this vision of the Oneness of Life has dawned, and who are imbued with the spirit of unity, steadily increases. They are to be found everywhere, in homes, in business, in factories, in the professions, in Municipal Councils and Parliaments and in International Organisations. They are to be regarded as the potential saviours of mankind, threatened as it now is with atomic and bacteriological warfare waged by means of guided missiles. Such weapons are already available. In consequence, no place on earth can now be safeguarded against sudden, total destruction. In the presence of these terrible possibilities, those who work for world unity are as the little leaven that leaveneth the whole. In them, mental development has reached that most important phase which enables them to perceive unity amidst diversity—the first of my three ideas. In consequence, they fully accept the noble *dictum* recently enunciated by Professor Einstein: " Each man is here for the sake of the other men." Whether consciously or unconsciously, they exert a pressure in the direction of co-ordination and harmonious co-operation in the cause of human welfare. Herein, I submit, lies the heart of the problem of world freedom, namely, *in the minds and in the motive for living of individual men and women.*

The True Enemies of Mankind

Unhappily, there is another and darker side to the present world situation. Selfish and unscrupulous individuals in their turn combine into groups, in order ruthlessly to exploit their fellow men for their own personal profit. Such people also exist in homes, in business, in factories, in the professions, in Municipal Councils and Parliaments and in International Organisations. These selfish men are the initiators and wagers of class warfare, as also of industrial, financial and political warfare. They are inflexible, determined to obtain for themselves and their groups the largest possible share of world power and wealth. One glaring example of their methods is the destruction of greatly needed food to boost prices.

Thus, as I have already said, humanity at this most critical time is divided into two classes of people. On the one hand there are those who have perceived the truth of unity and, having outgrown the passion for personal power and possessions, have seriously dedicated their lives to the service of their fellow men. On the other hand there exist the dark fanatics of selfishness, the ruthless individualists who acknowledge no god but self and no goal but self-interest, and pursue that goal relentlessly. If these men hear a voice of conscience or see a light of idealism, they silence the one and scorn the other. It is these people who cause the U. N. to be impotent to prevent war and who delay the attainment of world peace.

Self-reform the Key

We have now come to the heart of the problem—our personal contribution. As citizens of the world, in what way have we also failed? What could you and I have done since the founding of the United Nations to bring about world peace? What can we still do? Can we help or can we hinder? Definitely we can either help or hinder; for if the historical process leading to the birth of one world—of free peoples, please remember—is to be quickened, that quickening can only come when a sufficient number of men and women in the free Nations desire it, think it, seek it and diligently work for it. Someone has very truly said: "Peace begins with the United Nations, but the United Nations begins with you." There, I suggest, lies the responsibility of every thoughtful individual, challenging him to hold the ideal of world co-operation in mind, to study its basis and its method, and to live it out in the world of his own life.

This, I believe, is axiomatic; for the regeneration of human society depends very largely upon the regeneration of the individual. The world problem is the individual problem. A person who is at war with himself, his conscience, his family and his fellow citizens, cannot be a peacemaker in the world. Humanity's problem is not only to co-ordinate Races and Nations and to improve the lot of man as an economic unit of world society. It is also necessary for the individual to improve his own self-knowledge and his ability to live in harmony with his fellows as an informed, effective and humane member of his community. A measure of peace within is essential to a positive contribution to peace without. All true reform begins with self-reform.

Thus, as ever, the would-be reformer is confronted with the greatest single contribution that he can make, namely, the reformation of himself. However helpless we may feel ourselves to be amidst what Mr. Churchill called "the tides and tornadoes of world events", nothing stands in the way of immediate self-reform.

The responsibility, then, is our own. We cannot wash our hands of it. Pontius Pilate washed his hands and the world has never forgiven him. Recognition of responsibility, co-operativeness and the spirit of sharing in individual life and character—these inner attributes will most surely produce their outward and visible results. The living stones of which the temple of the new civilisation must be built will consist of voluntarily co-operative individuals.

The Brotherhood of Man

I close with a statement of a personal conviction. As one who has been travelling throughout the world for the last thirty years, meeting the peoples who live in many lands, who speak many languages and who wear skins of differing colours, I have gradually found myself obliged to recognise that below the surface of these outer differences amongst men there exist the unity and the solidarity of the whole human Race on earth. All people experience much the same hopes, sorrows and joys. Sages and philosophers tell us that all men come forth from one single, Divine Source, are members of one spiritual Race which is without division of any kind. The truth about the Races of men on earth, I have come to believe, is that they are in fact all one, one brotherhood, one family, with one purpose and one goal. As a poet has said: " All are parts of one stupendous whole ".

The answer to one of the questions with which I began—what is ahead of us, a Third World War or a stable peace?—could be, and I hope *will* be, " enduring world peace ". World unity—a universal brotherhood of free men—*is*, I submit, attainable on earth, the reason being that human brotherhood is not a condition to be created; it is a fact in Nature to be recognised, to be acknowledged and to be ratified in all human relationships, as one day it will be. Whether this establishment of world co-operation comes soon or late depends, as I have said, very largely upon you and upon me, upon our thoughts, our motives for living and our daily lives.

Thus, we have come full circle from the world to the individual and from the individual back to the world. As the individual grows out of his own selfishness, so will the world grow out of the danger of enslavement into freedom and enduring peace.

* * * * *

The question whether it is practicable for modern man, almost submerged as he is in the pressing task of earning a living, to live according to such ideals as are here presented, is considered in the next broadcast.

CHAPTER II

HOW THE MAN IN THE WORLD MAY LIVE THE SPIRITUAL LIFE

The Monastic Life

SINCE, as stated in the preceding broadcast, the world problem is the individual problem, and both safety from a Third World War and moral and spiritual progress of humanity depend upon an increase in the influence and number of spiritually minded, dedicated men and women, the questions must be considered: Is it possible to respond to idealism amidst mundane duties? Can the spiritual life be lived by those of us who are busy people out in the world? To these questions Theosophy answers " yes ", and adds that one general key to success in this endeavour is the conscientious fulfilment of duty; for duty well done, I suggest, is the most perfect expression of religion.

Theosophy goes further, however, and says that a spiritual mode of life is not only possible but is, for those attracted to it, the surest way to happiness. It also acknowledges the value of the contemplative life and the work of the Religious Orders. They have their very important place in the training, the purification and the dedication of mind and heart to the service of God. Indeed, the reincarnationist would tell us that it is part of the scheme of human development occasionally to have a life as a monk, a nun, a hermit, or some other kind of recluse. In retreat, away from the stress, the strain and the temptations of life, we are able to concentrate upon the deep, eternal truths, to seek and find the solution of life's many mysteries, and to awaken powers of spiritual perception. But in this Twentieth Century life of ours many of us find ourselves out in the world and confronted by the innumerable problems inseparable from the tasks and duties of busy men and women. Nevertheless, each one of us is essentially a divine being and spirituality ought to be—and one day will be—our natural state.

What is Spirituality?

Spirituality, then, simply consists of discovering and becoming one's Higher Self. The spiritual life is one in which the noblest in us is accentuated in motives, thoughts, feelings and words, as also, especially, in the conduct of life. Indeed, it might truly be said that the discovery and the expression of one's Higher Self is the immediate, the main and the true purpose of our existence here in the flesh. Pain, from which we naturally shrink and wish to safeguard others, can be seen to have a certain value in human experience, for it can serve as a spur urging us to search for and discover our own divine nature.

Pain the Teacher

The message of pain is, however, at least threefold. Suffering comes to all of us. It can be used to awaken in us compassion for the pain of others—and to be compassionate, remember, is to be spiritual. Second, pain can teach us to live according to the law of love, which we have failed to do, and in that failure have produced our unhappiness under the law of cause and effect. Third, as I have already said, it can be used to spur us to rise to those levels of our nature and consciousness where pain is not, which means the level of permanent realities and of our own higher, Spiritual Selves. Thus exalted, we can release into our lives the power, the light and the life of our divine nature. Then spirituality will become natural to us.

How is all this to be done by busy men and women amidst the pressure of earthly life and duties? Two of the essentials are said to be interior, spiritual awakening and ordered effort. The interior awakening is perfectly natural; it corresponds in man to the appearance of bud and flower in the plant, when a certain stage of development has been attained. This awakening is generally accompanied by a vision of divine perfection and a spontaneous choice of a way of life in which the spiritual rules the material in man. This inner experience comes in different ways to different people. Sometimes it is purely intellectual. To find answers to the pressing problems of life, to discover a religious belief founded on logic, and to be utterly assured of the justice of God—these become urgent necessities. As a result of this inward pressure, the great search for knowledge is begun.

Aspiration

A second effect of spiritual awakening has been described as "a divine discontent" and as "the inexpressible longing of the inner man for the Infinite". This longing is often born of dissatisfaction with oneself, of self-shame and a sense of failure, even amidst worldly success. The aspirant sees how selfishness and sheer materialism have ruled his life, how hurtful he has been to others, and he now seeks to eliminate these faults from his character.

The Creed of Kinship

A third experience often associated with this mental change is that of a growing sense of kinship with all other beings, which is accompanied by a profound feeling of responsibility for their welfare. Great changes can come out of this experience. The motive for living alters from getting to giving, from living for the personal, smaller self to serving the universal, larger Self—God and one's fellow men. A great kindliness generally begins to show itself at this stage. Sometimes a Cause for human welfare is adopted, and the spirit of dedication takes up its abode within the heart of the spiritually awakened man. All of this interior experience can be quite unforced, natural and utterly sincere.

Then, sooner or later, a seemingly strange but quite natural phenomenon occurs. An answer comes to the cry of the heart for knowledge and help in spiritual attainment. Often quite unexpectedly, and as if by chance, information in an acceptable form is made available, in a book, a pamphlet, a few remarks in the course of conversation, a lecture, or even in a vision or a dream. If the search for truth is steadfastly continued, a senior in the spiritual life is met and he or she offers practical guidance in finding and treading the Path of Discipleship.

In order to assure, and even hasten, this most fortunate discovery of a teacher, it is advisable to make a sincere gesture of both service to others and renunciation of some undesirable indulgence. A spiritual call or prayer should also be sent up for help in becoming a really effective servant of God and of all mankind. An answer is assured, for every human being is continually watched over with loving care. Such, in part, is the experience of interior awakening and such are some of its results.

The Contemplative Life

The second essential to success in the dedicated life is, as I have said, ordered effort. The spiritual life is, in fact, a science. Three things have to be done: regular, daily meditation or prayer, study and character building, self-giving in service. Meditation is based upon the fact that all that we need of spiritual power, wisdom and knowledge is within us, is indeed, part of our Inner Self. We must find that Self and learn daily to draw down inspiration and strength from the highest aspect of our nature. Day by day, a quarter of an hour or so should be saved for quiet contemplation and for the inward search for truth, power and peace.

As a result of regular meditation, one can come to know one's Self as a radiant, immortal, divine being, a flame which is part of the fire of God. This aspiration to the spiritual heights has been beautifully expressed in the words: "Ask, and it shall be given you; seek, and ye shall find; knock, and it shall be opened unto you."[1] But, be it remembered, one must ask, seek and knock *with a will*.

Practical Idealism

The problem still remains of the application of this idealism to one's daily living. This is far from being impossible, though admittedly difficult at times. Let us, then, try and see how members of various professions and businesses might possibly apply spiritual ideals to their daily life and work. If one is a doctor, for example, then one's profession can be regarded, as it is by many physicians, as a divine vocation. Filled with compassion for the suffering of man, the dedicated physician will perform all ministrations as an agent of the Great Healer of the World and in the hope that His healing grace may reach the sufferers who come for aid. The teacher, too, may regard himself as a servant of the God within the pupil and the scholar. The Government Official can sink desire for personal progress and undue enrichment in an effort to obtain the

[1] *Matt.* VII. 7.

ideal administration for his department and for the country as a whole. The lawyer can, as many do, become the guide, the philosopher and the friend of the family, one to whom all can go for direction and friendly counsel in time of need. Homemakers—wives and mothers—can make of their homes centres of love, beauty, order and peace. Some homes *are* centres of spirituality, culture and beauty, the work of the house being done in the spirit of service to those who will use the home.

Thus, indeed, it *is* practicable to live a spiritual life amidst the pressure of worldly duties. The field of service is just where we are and the devoted fulfilment of duty constitutes the dedicated life. So it is not a change of activity or kind of work that is needed, but rather a change of accent or motive for carrying out that activity. Finally, I repeat, this inner awakening and self-consecration to noble deeds come from *within* the Soul. The change is therefore perfectly natural, quite spontaneous. As Tagore so beautifully said: " He who can open the bud does it so simply."

* * * * *

Some of the ideas in this and the preceding broadcast were also presented in the form of the following duologue between a visitor from another planet and a citizen of this world. The fact that the subject of Flying Saucers was much to the fore at the time of its transmission added topical interest to this form of presentation.

CHAPTER III

THE TRAGIC CAUSES OF INTERNATIONAL DISCORD

A DUOLOGUE

VISITOR. (*A friendly person, newly arrived from another planet.*) How do you do?

EARTHMAN. (*Not very sure of himself and his world.*) How are you?

V. Well, thank you. Understand you have been having some trouble here for the last forty years or so?

E. Very serious trouble.

V. Wars, I believe?

E. Yes, wars—amongst other things.

V. Do you begin to see daylight yet?

E. Yes, I think we do.

V. I'm glad to hear that. From what direction is the daylight coming?

E. We've formed an International Union of fifty Nations.

V. You expect much from that Organisation?

E. Oh, yes. The member Nations are now pledged to arbitrate instead of fight.

V. How long ago was that?

E. About seven years now, though we did have another League some twenty years before that.

V. About seven years! May I then report back that war has now ceased on Earth and our help won't be needed?

E. Er—not exactly.

V. Why not? Isn't the Union working?

E. Er—no, not very well. In fact, we've got two wars on now—both of them in Asia, by the way.

V. But why don't the fifty Nations in your Union tell the combatants to stop?

E. It's not as simple as all that. You see, one member of the Union, nearly the strongest, is helping an aggressor Nation with weapons and munitions. Without this help, the aggressor would have been defeated a long time ago by the other members of the Union.

V. Do you mean to say that the Union itself is fighting?

E. Yes, it is. It has to in order to prevent an aggressor from overrunning a weaker Nation.

V. Why don't the people of the United Nations individually combine and stop these two wars?

E. The people are rather busy, as a matter of fact.

V. Busy! Doing what?

E. Oh—earning money in order to get food and other things. They can't help themselves, can they?

V. I suppose they can't, but do they earn their money honestly and according to the principles of the International Union?

E. Not always, I'm afraid. At least, some do, but many don't.

V. Do they help each other to earn money for food? What I want you to tell me is whether the ideal of the Union of Nations is lived out in the daily lives of the people of the member Nations?

E. Er—as a matter of fact—er—

V. Come on, man. As individual persons, are the people of the United Nations helping each other to get money for food and in their private lives, or are they not?

E. Er—no, they're not actually. They do socially, but "each for himself and the Devil take the hindmost" is their business motto. Industry must go on, you know.

V. I suppose it must; but about industry. Do the employers and the employees co-operate with each other for the good of the industry? Do they work together like a happy family?

E. Er—no. Not exactly like a happy family.

V. Why not?

E. Well, after all, one must look after oneself, you know. Some employers want maximum production with minimum expense. Some employees want maximum pay for minimum hours of work.

V. What a peculiar method of working! Then there is actually a sort of warfare within industry itself?

E. Yes—there is. But I suppose that is inevitable, isn't it?

V. Why should it be inevitable? Don't the employers and the employees see that the World Union can't work unless there is unity amongst the various classes and peoples of your world?

E. Yes, they see that, if they think at all, but I guess it's "self first" with most of them. They try to defeat competitors in business and so earn more money for themselves.

V. But, don't they see that if some people are poor, and therefore hungry, everybody else must suffer, since we are all one?

E. No, they don't; besides, self-interest is forced upon them by the economic situation. But when you say "*we* are all one", do you include yourself with us?

V. Of course. Why not?

E. Well—you and your people live rather a long distance away, don't you?

V. Oh, no, not very far; only a few hours at the speed of interplanetary travel. Besides, human brotherhood is universal. It bridges space and unites planets, just as, here on Earth, it unites continents, races and persons.

E. What a strange idea! A universal brotherhood extending from planet to planet!

V. It must be so. If unity is true anywhere in the Universe—here on Earth, for example—and it is true, then it must be true everywhere. Doesn't humanity on this Earth know that?

E. No, I am afraid they don't—at least, not many people.

V. Well, human brotherhood is universal wherever man exists. But to come back to our subject of industry. How about the trade between Nations? Is that co-operative?

E. No, it's highly competitive. In fact, Nations trade with enemy Nations, even during wars. Traders form monopolies, fix prices, and restrain trade between States and foreign countries, although they know very well that others will starve in consequence.

V. Why do Governments and businessmen restrain trade?

E. In order to make people pay more for their goods. They even destroy food in order to keep up prices. Industry must go on, you know. Some keen businessmen make huge fortunes in the drug traffic, from white slavery, by selling alcoholic liquor, and by killing animals for sport.

V. Killing animals for sport! Haven't they any consideration for the sufferings of the animals they make sport of? And don't they know about cause and effect?

E. We have been told.

V. Hasn't anybody made it plain to you, though, that anyone who kills unnecessarily gets killed himself.

E. Yes, I suppose they have, but it's hard to believe, isn't it?

V. It is very obvious to us, inescapable, in fact. But these traders you speak of: if what you say is true, they are all waging war against their fellow men and against the animal kingdom for their own profit and pleasure.

E. Er—yes, they are, now you mention it.

V. How, then, can they expect the International Union to work? You yourself can surely see that continual private and commercial warfare is bound to lead to military warfare.

E. Er—yes. I suppose it is; in fact, it has already done so.

V. So that—correct me if I am wrong—on the one hand you form a Union of Nations to prevent international war, and on the other you continually wage private warfare against each other and against your animals?

E. Yes, we do, if you put it like that. Of course, there are a great many good and kind people on earth.

V. Then why don't they do something about this tragic contradiction?

E. They would like to, but they are so hopelessly in the minority that they are rather ineffective as yet. Any effort they make is sort of swamped by sheer numbers and habit and custom and, as the saying goes, " that's business ".

V. Earth people seem to place a very high value on business. Haven't you organised your production and distribution so that they meet the needs of Nations and peoples and districts?

E. Er—no. I'm afraid we haven't. It wouldn't be competitive enough, you see, and it's competition which keeps business going. Then there is something else which we have that I think I must explain to you. It is called power politics, and this colours almost all our international relationships. In spite of the existence of the Union, many political philosophers place much reliance on force and cunning. They say: " Let him take who has the power and let him keep who can." Such people believe that the honour, morality and goodwill which you have been talking about are only useful methods, which must give way to force and cunning when the real interests between the Nations clash.

V. Don't the businessmen of your planet have any morality at all?

E. I'm afraid they haven't, particularly where business is concerned.

V. It seems to me that business on Earth is more important to you than either morality or peace on Earth. Don't you have any religion at all?

E. Er—yes, we have a kind of religion but it doesn't seem to help very much—except, of course, some individuals. You see, the Christian Religion itself is divided into about three hundred different Sects, and they won't co-operate very much with each other. In fact, we have competition in religious matters also.

V. I see. So you have warfare right in the realm of religion itself? That is very serious indeed. Those of use who have been visiting you recently spoke very truly.

E. Is it better, then, where you have come from?

V. Oh, yes. We believe that each man exists for the sake of the other men. That's our working basis.

E. "Each man exists for the sake of the other men." That's rather hard to understand, isn't it?

V. We think it's obvious and so, apparently, do the founders of your International Union. Surely, the whole idea of your United Nations is based upon a sense of mutual responsibility. That, of course, is your greatest hope; for if the United Nations succeeds, then the worst of your international troubles are behind you.

E. (*Staring at V.*) Could you, perhaps, explain our troubles a little more fully? Why is it we're in such a bad way?

V. I could explain, but I don't think you'd understand. It would be a mere jumble of words to you, I'm afraid.

E. Oh, please try. I'd like just to hear the words. Why are we in such trouble?

V. Well, it's partly the contradictions you've told me about—forming a Union of Nations and, at the same time, fighting each other as individuals—and partly because of two other things. The first of these is—and here are those words that I told you about—that you are in the Fourth Chain of your Planetary Scheme and in its Fourth Round. You are also on the Fourth Globe and in its fourth racial epoch. Now, the fourth phase of all cycles is the lowest and the densest and the most material, and just now you are right at the deepest point.

E. (*doubtfully*) Er—thank you very much. How enlightening! What is the second reason then?

V. That you are *also* in a mental age. You are just learning to use the analytical mind. You see diversity, but you cannot yet perceive unity. This temporarily prevents you from realising the fact that all men belong to one spiritual Race, which is without division of any kind.

E. One spiritual Race without divisions of any kind! How wonderful! Please go on.

V. Now, the mind is essentially analytical, separative, acquisitive and possessive. So, put these two things together—the Fourth Race on the Fourth Globe of the Fourth Round of the Fourth Chain *and* the accentuation of the formal, analytical mind—and there you are.

E. I see. Then how long is our trouble likely to last, do you think?

V. You *are* round the corner. You are now in the Fifth Race. That is why you have been able to conceive an International Union and *that* is your greatest hope.

E. Thank you. I am glad to hear that the worst is *behind* us. How long will it be, do you think, before we have a lasting peace?

V. I fear the problem will still be with you until war itself, or at least the threat of war, forces you to face the facts and to reason from them.

E. What facts especially?

V. As I have been saying—you must be consistent. For instance, you can't fight against each other all the time in business, in industry and in religion and at the same time have world peace. World union cannot be attained until a sufficient number of individuals actually live out unity, brotherhood and peace in the world of their own lives. But I'm afraid I must be off. (*Moves towards airship.*)

E. Please don't go. I do wish more people had heard what you have said. After all I'm only one. What can I do?

V. A very great deal. You can become a unifier and a co-operator in your own home, in your own neighbourhood and city. You, the private citizen, are an extremely important person.

E. (*hesitatingly*) Am I? Well, I will try. But why are you going?

V. To try and get help, of course. You will think over what I have said, won't you? Especially that the effort of a single individual to live as a unifier is of immense importance.

E. Yes, I'll remember.

V. Splendid! Goodbye.

E. Goodbye.

* * * * *

The following Hymn expresses the Theosophical teaching of the Universal Brotherhood of Man so effectively that, although not broadcast, it is here added:—

"Gather us in, Thou Love that fillest all!
Gather our rival faiths within Thy fold!
Rend each man's temple-veil and bid it fall,
That we may know that Thou has been of old:
Gather us in.

"Gather us in: we worship only Thee;
In varied names we stretch a common hand;
In diverse forms a common soul we see;
In many ships we seek one spirit-land:
Gather us in.

"Each sees one colour of Thy rainbow-light,
Each looks upon one tint and calls it heaven;
Thou art the fullness of our partial sight;
We are not perfect till we find the seven:
Gather us in.

"Thine is the mystic life great India craves,
Thine is the Parsee's sin-destroying beam,
Thine is the Buddhist's rest from tossing waves,
Thine is the empire of vast China's dream:
Gather us in.

"Thine is the Roman's strength without his pride,
Thine is the Greek's glad world without its slaves,
Thine is Judea's law, with love beside,
The truth that censures and the grace that saves:
Gather us in.

"Some seek a Father in the heavens above,
Some ask a human image to adore,
Some crave a Spirit vast as life and love;
Within Thy mansions we have all and more:
Gather us in."

—REV. GEORGE MATHESON, 1842-1906.

CHAPTER IV

MEDITATION AND THE POWER IT BESTOWS

Voices from the Past

THALES, the ancient Greek philosopher, sometimes called the Sage of Miletus, was asked by a Sophist and answered the following nine questions:—

What is the oldest of all things? God, because He has always existed.

What is the most beautiful of all things? The universe, because it is the work of God.

What is the greatest of things? Space, because it contains all that has been created.

What is the most constant of all things? Hope, because it still remains with man after he has lost everything else.

What is the best of all things? Freedom, because without it there is nothing good.

What is the quickest of all things? Thought, because in less than a minute it can fly to the end of the universe.

What is the strongest of all things? Necessity, which makes man face all the dangers of life.

What is the easiest of all things? To give advice.
What is the most difficult of all things? To know thyself.

The Pathway to Power

Whilst many problems confront the human Race as a whole, every individual is faced with his or her own problem of self-discovery, of the attainment of serenity, enduring happiness, and peace of mind and heart. The Sage of Miletus was right; the most difficult of all things is to know oneself. The Kingdom of Heaven, it has been said, is within us. Therefore the power, the happiness and the peace which we are all seeking must also be within us. How to find this power and happiness and peace, how to become aware of our own divine nature and of the divine Presence within us, how to find God and live consciously in His presence, in His service and in the service of the human Race—these are pressing human problems.

The Way to God

What has Theosophy to contribute to their solution? It recognises the value of at least three approaches to the source and the centre of Divine Power within each one of us. The first of these is the personal approach to God through prayer, particularly in times of need. Love for a parent is instinctual in man. It is natural, therefore, as well as very wise, frequently to turn to the Spiritual Parent of all men; for, whilst human parents die and pass beyond our reach, He can never disappear.

Such sincere and earnest prayers are always answered, though not necessarily in the way expected. It has been truly said that more things are wrought by prayer than this world dreams of, and if to potential words we add potent acts and make the atmosphere within and without us pure and divine, then the God within can act outwardly. Then we can help ourselves and others; we can even perform seeming miracles.

"Ardent Prayer Opens Heaven"[1]

Prayer turns and attunes the mind and the heart to the omnipresent, Divine Life, Love, Light and Power. The Lord's Prayer is a splendid example of such effective means of supplication, as are many other prayers in the Scriptures and Prayer Books of the Christian Faith. Prayer does not always mean supplication and petition, however, but also adoration and a reaching up towards the Supreme Source of Life; for it is possible to rise on the wings of devotion and adoration to the very heart of Divine Love and, on occasion, to feel and know the unfailing Presence of God.

By means of regular prayer, heart and mind become sensitised to this Presence, which can be felt as a consoling and inspiring power. Indeed, one can come to know that in very truth the everlasting arms are always underneath. Such, in part, is the way of prayer.

Congregational Worship

A second approach to God is through congregational worship as in temple, cathedral and church, and also

[1] *Night*, Young.

in family prayers. These can prove most effective for certain temperaments, for it is often easier to be uplifted when aspiring with a group of like-minded people than when one is alone.

The Still, Small Voice

Meditation constitutes a third way to realisation of the Divine and the attainment of spiritual power. This is the individual approach to God in love and aspiration, asking nought from Him but only seeking to realise oneness with Him. We *can* become consciously one with the very highest Deity; for even the Causeless Cause has Its shrine and altar on the holy and untrodden ground of the human heart. Although God is naturally invisible, He may be known and heard as the still, small voice of our own spiritual consciousness. Those who worship thus do so in the sanctified solitude of their own Souls, making their Spirit the only mediator between themselves and the Universal Spirit, their good actions the only priests. This way is open to those who are spiritually awakened and who experience what Ruysbroeck, the great Flemish mystic, called "the hunger for God". These most surely find, for truly the Divine Life and Divine Intelligence are within each one of us. They are, in fact, the reality of our existence, our Spiritual Soul.

Laws Governing Self-Illumination

How may this become personal experience? Theosophy answers, by three means which are: changing when necessary the motive of life from selfishness to selflessness and the mode of life from self-indulgence to self-restraint, and by regular meditation.

How does one meditate? Let me describe an effective method of gaining self-illumination by means of regular, daily contemplation of God. To achieve this a certain time must be set aside each day. A period of quietude must be arranged for, preferably in the morning, for then the brain should be rested, the mind reasonably quiet, whilst the occult forces which make for enlightenment are on the increase.

It has been said that God knocks at the door of the heart of man once in every twenty-four hours. Often we fail to hear this "knocking" of One who continually seeks entrance into our lives, not because we are not seeking, but because we are so busy with the necessary duties of the day. If, however, we can set aside some ten minutes or a quarter of an hour every day, when we can silence heart and mind and turn our thoughts towards the Source of our existence, then the Divine Presence can make Itself known to us. Daily, alone and in quietude, we must open the door of our hearts that God may enter in. Privacy is necessary for full success, for to be suddenly intruded upon when one is abstracted in thought is to run the risk of nervous shock and strain. These can be avoided by ensuring complete seclusion during meditation.

Correct Posture

Much has been said and written concerning the appropriate posture for meditation. In the East where the science of *Yoga*, or union with God, is taught and practised, numerous postures are advised. For ordinary purposes, however, it is only necessary that the body should be completely relaxed and the spine straight, preferably erect. Physical relaxation, in its effect on meditation, might be compared to the careful engagement of the first unit of the zipper, which makes the rest of the series of hooks engage smoothly.

Ideally, the breathing should be slowed down to half the normal speed, but breathing exercises with the thought concentrated upon some centre in the body are not necessary and, indeed, can be dangerous. The effort to meditate must be regular, whether results are noticed or not, for as Nietszche said, " In the mountains of truth you never climb in vain. Either you reach a higher point today or you exercise your strength in order to be able to climb higher tomorrow." Therefore, once having begun try to keep on, for it is regularity and constant repetition which contribute so largely to success.

Suitable Themes

These external matters attended to, the thought should be fixed upon some great truth; for example, the omnipresent, Divine Life, the Oneness of all Life, or the unity of the Spirit of man with the Spirit of the Universe, which is God. These truths should be dwelt upon, contemplated, until personal realisation of them begins to be attained. Beautiful Scriptural texts expressing them may well be chosen as aids to concentration, particularly at first. For those Christians who find concentration difficult, the more joyous and beautiful scenes in the life of Our Lord may be mentally pictured. The details may be filled in and the Divine Figure Itself clearly visualised. Love and adoration may then with all reverence be offered to Him, as the aspirant seeks to "touch the hem of His garment" and later to become one with Him and live in His very presence. Then, as has been beautifully said,[1] there will descend into the still heart "the sweet rain of new inward consolation and the heavenly dew of the sweetness of God." Members of other Faiths may similarly contemplate the lives of Those who founded them.

A Technique of Self-Illumination

An effective method of meditation is consciously to dissociate oneself, first from the physical body, next from the emotions and then from the mind, finally affirming one's own divinity and unity with the Divine in all. In this method, also, concentration may be aided by means of such mental affirmations as: "I am the Divine Self, eternal, immortal, indestructible, radiant with Spiritual Light." "I am that Self of Light, that Self am I." "The Self in me is one with the Self in all." "I am that Self, that Self am I." Before passing from one affirmation to its successor, a pause should be observed to permit contemplation and realisation of the truth which has been affirmed. By this third means—private meditation and

[1] Ruysbroeck.

contemplation—the Soul may be lifted up into the realisation of its own inner splendour and of its unity with the One Supreme Splendour of All.

As great mental and spiritual heights can be reached by contemplating one's unity with God, the return to physical awareness should not be sudden. The centre of consciousness should be deliberately brought down—speaking diagrammatically—first into the mind, then, after a brief pause into the emotions, and finally, into the brain and body. This should be followed by a few moments of physical rest and self-adjustment before taking up the duties of life.

Light, more Light

As a further help to those who seek to acquire the technique of meditation—which has been described as a " knack "—here is a brief description of what may be expected when the centre of consciousness is elevated into union with the Immortal Soul, the Ego, which is the Spiritual Self of man. Mystics and seers unite in testifying to an entry into a brilliant and supernal light, the light " which never was on land or sea ". The centre of self-awareness and of observation is as a more brilliant focus of light within a vast and shoreless sea in which other such centres, representing the Egoic Selves of other beings, are to be seen. Then a great intensity of existence and activity, combined with perfect equipoise and ease, is experienced. Yet there is no sense of either effort or resistance, duality having been reduced to a minimum. Such experiences as those of treasured friendship returned, love fully reciprocated and complete comprehension of a truth, a work of art or another Ego, also characterise Egoic consciousness, but in greatly heightened degree.

From Doubt to Certainty

Uttermost certainty concerning the immortality and indestructibility of the true Self and of the purpose of human existence, which is evolution to the stature of the perfect man, as also of the fact of the unity of all Life and the family relationship with all living beings—these are known by every reasonably evolved Ego as fundamental verities. Bereavement, separation, loss of loved ones, are impossible at this level of consciousness where neither time nor space can limit the free play of the human intellect. Mutual Egoic attunement with certain other members of the human family, and especially with those who have become particularly beloved, provides complete assurance of unbroken unity with them throughout all time.

The Inner Ruler Immortal

The Ego of man, then, knows itself to be an eternal, immortal and indestructible centre of Divine Power, Life and Light. These well up within it as from an inexhaustible Source and shine all about it as a glowing radiance, bright with many hues. This, in small part, is the condition of consciousness of the Spiritual Self of man.

PART SIX

THE LAWS OF HEALTH AND HAPPINESS

CHAPTER I

THE INFLUENCE OF MIND AND EMOTION ON HEALTH AND DISEASE

The Spectre of Disease

WHY is it that, although rapid progress is being made in many branches of science, medical science fails successfully to prevent and to cure many diseases? Why are the incidence and the mortality of so many diseases on the increase today? Why do not advances in diagnosis, development of more and more intricate and sensitive instruments, and remarkable progress in surgery and hospital techniques, bring to mankind increasing immunity from sickness and more certain methods of treatment and cure?

The Sickness of Man

A great physician, Dr. Bircher-Benner, has stated these problems as follows: " Although sanitation, hygiene and dietetics have reduced mortality and lengthened the average duration of life, statistics demonstrate that the general ill-health and proneness to disease of mankind are on the increase. A growing sickliness is showing itself among modern civilised humanity. Every individual and every family are continually faced with the possibility that mental or physical, and often moral, disease will strike them. Disabling and painful diseases and epidemics are the almost certain lot of present-day man." [1]

What is the Theosophical contribution to this problem of the increasing sickliness of modern man, despite the great advances on almost every other frontier of science? That contribution consists of knowledge, particularly of two facts in Nature. One of these is the existence of a law of cause and effect, action and reaction, or compensation. The other fact is that man is a sevenfold being made up of Will, Wisdom, Intelligence, mentality, emotion, vital energy and a physical body, and that interaction between these various parts is continually occurring.

The Law of Cause and Effect

Let us look at these two ideas. The law of cause and effect is described as the law inherent in the nature of things, the ultimate law of the Universe, the source, the fount, the origin of all other laws under which effects follow causes. In the East this law is called *karma*; it is said to operate continuously upon man, every one of whose actions produces an appropriate reaction. This operation of the law is, however, modified by later actions from hour to hour, from day to day and from life to life. Applying this teaching to the problem of disease, it may well be said that persistent selfishness

[1] *Children's Diet.*

and cruelty bring disease and sorrow, whilst love and service bring health and happiness. This knowledge, simple though it may sound, is regarded by some as the very heart of the science of health and happiness. Our Lord would seem to have supported this view of disease, for after healing the helpless man of Bethesda He said to him "sin no more",[1] as if to imply that the root cause was sinning and the sure prevention was to cease from sinning.

The answer to the problems of the universality of human suffering, and of the strange selectivity under which some suffer and others do not, is thus provided by knowledge of the operation of an exact law of cause and effect, or sowing and reaping, as St. Paul expressed it, for he said: "God is not mocked: for whatsoever a man soweth, that shall he also reap."[2]

Interaction between Soul and Body

The second Theosophical idea which may be applied to the solution of the problem of health and disease concerns, as I have said, the continual interaction between the Spirit, the mind and the emotions of man on the one hand, and his physical body on the other. Dr. Alexis Carrel in his wonderful book, *Man the Unknown*,[3] describes this interaction as follows: "Envy, hate, fear, when these sentiments are habitual, are capable of starting organic changes and genuine diseases.

[1] *John* V. 14.
[2] *Gal.* VI. 7.
[3] Published by Hamish Hamilton Ltd., 90 Great Russell St., London, 1935.

Moral suffering profoundly disturbs health. Business-men who do not know how to fight worry, die young. . .

" Emotions. . . determine the dilation or the contraction of the small arteries, through the vasomotor nerves. They are, therefore, accompanied by changes in the circulation of the blood in tissues and organs. Pleasure causes the skin of the face to flush. Anger and fear turn it white. . . . The affective states. . . . stimulate or stop the (gland) secretions, or modify their chemical constitution. It has been proved that a mora shock may cause marked changes in the blood. Thought can generate organic lesions. The instability of modern life, the ceaseless agitation and the lack of security create states of consciousness which bring about nervous and organic disorders of the stomach and of the intestines, defective nutrition, and passage of intestinal microbes into the circulatory apparatus. . . . (Various) infections of the kidney and bladder are the remote results of mental and moral unbalance. Such diseases are almost unknown in social groups where life is simpler and not so agitated, where anxiety is less constant. . . . Likewise, those who keep the peace of their inner self in the midst of tumult are immune from nervous and organic disorders . . . Man thinks, invents, loves, suffers, admires and prays with his brain and all his organs." So wrote Dr. Alexis Carrel.

A New Branch of Medicine

As a result of the progress of medical research in this direction, a relatively new and most interesting branch of medicine, called psychosomatic medicine, has now come into existence. The word " psychosomatic " is derived from the Greek words *psyche*, meaning mind or Soul, and *soma*, the body. This new attitude recognises the fact, which Theosophy has always taught, that the human being is complex and mysterious, a creature whose thoughts, emotions, brain and tissues are constantly reacting one upon the other.

The literature on this subject points out that we do some things deliberately. We run, work or eat by our own will. We decide to wash the breakfast dishes, but we do not decide to blush with embarrassment or double our heartbeat with rage. These actions are controlled by the involuntary or automatic nervous system. Such deep feelings as hate, fear and the need for love, of which we may be wholly unconscious at the time, can find bodily expression through this involuntary system.

If a mother is worried over her children's health or is afraid they are not getting along well in school, she may have an attack of indigestion. She suffers from an upset stomach because she is depressed and anxious. If she continues for a sufficient period of time thus to make herself ill, real danger to the tissues may ensue. A person with a possibly serious gastro-intestinal complaint may go to a doctor. He may find that the illness is caused by emotional tension whereupon, if he practises psychosomatic medicine, he would not only treat the physical ailment but would also look for the cause in the patient's mental or emotional structure, and in his relationship with his environment.

Physicians of Souls

As further progress in this direction is made, it would seem that the function of the physician will undergo a change, or rather be greatly extended. A ministering, almost a priestly, vocation will have to be added to that of the practice of medicine or surgery as known today. There are already indications of a recognition of this necessity; for more and more physicians have indeed come to realise that many of the ills that beset the body are symptoms, not of some organic malfunctions which can be treated by medicine or surgery, but of some psychic or emotional disturbances which drugs or scalpels are incapable of reaching.

About one-third of the patients, it has been said, who come to physicians for treatment have no bodily disorder to account for their sicknesses. This estimate was made by Lieutenant-Colonel David M. Banen in a recent issue of the journal, *The Military Surgeon*. He went on to declare that another third of the patients, " while having demonstrable physical illness, have symptoms that at least in part are dependent upon emotional factors ".

When one realises the implications behind these cold statistics—that a great part of human illness is rooted in causes that cannot be adequately treated by an ordinary physician—then the picture becomes truly shocking. Psychiatry, psycho-analysis and the newly opened field of psychosomatic medicine are, indeed, partial answers to the now admitted limitations of traditional medical practice. Unfortunately, these three branches of medical science have only recently become recognised. Their practitioners are, as yet, able to cope with only a small fraction of the large number of sufferers; for, unlike the body, the human *psyche* or Soul does not readily lend itself to easy and quick diagnosis. Spiritual or emotional hurts cannot be detected by a fever thermometer. Yet the *psyche* is as real as the body and, if injured, may cause as much physical pain as a diseased kidney. It is not enough for a doctor to look upon a patient as an anatomical and physiological mechanism; he must also see him as a human being possessed of loves and hates, urges and passions, all of them capable of deeply disturbing both Soul and body. It is precisely because of this interaction that the spiritual understanding of a minister should be joined to the medical understanding of a doctor. There should also be added a thorough knowledge of the social and economic forces that act upon a patient's emotional and physical stability.

A Formula for Health and Happiness

I close with eight rules on the art of living given by Dr. John A. Schindler, Chief Physician of the Munroe Clinic in the State of Wisconsin, in the U. S. A.:—

1. Don't continually look for trouble.
2. Learn to like work, thus avoiding tension arising when work is disliked.

3. Have a hobby which gets your mind off the work tension. During work relax occasionally, and briefly, to think of the hobby.
4. Learn to like people. Avoid grudges against anyone, for this is disastrous. We have to live with people, so let us learn to like them.
5. Be satisfied when the situation is such that you cannot readily and easily change it. If you cannot easily adjust the situation, adjust yourself to it.
6. Learn to accept adversity. Don't let it defeat you. Don't brood on trouble and don't wallow in self-pity.
7. Learn to say the cheerful, humorous thing. Never say the mean or cruel thing. Help others to feel better and you will feel better yourself.
8. Meet problems with decision. Decide what you are going to do and then stop thinking about it.

By these means, says Dr. Schindler, harmful mental and emotional habits will be avoided and physical health be far more easily attained.

CHAPTER II

CRUELTY CAUSES DISEASE [1]

Humanity's Great Need

THE attainment and maintenance of perfect health is the intelligent person's supreme material pre-occupation. Health is the greatest physical necessity for every human being. Yet, despite the progress of modern science, the incidence of such diseases as leprosy, cancer, diabetes, hypertension and heart disease, and the mortality from them, tend to increase. More and larger hospitals, asylums, and prisons are continually having to be built.

How is this pressing problem, which now besets the whole human Race, to be solved? What are the fundamental laws governing health and well-being, and in what way is humanity so continually violating them that a perfectly and continually healthy individual is a rarity? In this broadcast I am going to offer an answer to these questions.

Unity, Harmony, Health

How may health be defined? I suggest that health is a condition of harmonious unity of ideal, thought,

[1] Acknowledgments are due to "The New Zealand Vegetarian" Magazine, in which the substance of this broadcast has appeared.

feeling and conduct. When this co-ordination of all the parts, spiritual, mental and physical, of a human being is achieved and maintained to a reasonable degree, two basic, inter-related laws are being obeyed. One is the law of harmony upon which, as equilibrium, the whole Universe is established, and the other is the law of compensation by which the whole Universe is ruled. When no natural law is violated, there can be no personal pain, although the consequences of all preceding transgressions will still have to be endured. When natural law *is* violated, suffering is inevitable. Moreover, the nature and the extent of the pain are always exactly proportionate to the degree of violation.

I am going to suggest that the application of this knowledge to the conduct of life, and obedience to these two laws of harmony and compensation, constitute the sole foundation upon which perfect health can be assured, perfect happiness can be maintained and, when they have been lost, both may be completely restored. Successful, final healing of the sick depends upon a return both to harmony and to obedience to natural law.

The Way to Happiness

Health may also be defined as the result of harmonious interplay between the forces of Spirit and mind on the one hand and their expression through emotion and physical action on the other. From above—actually from within—spiritual and mental forces and impulses play downwards into the outer man. From below, physical and emotional impulses both respond to and modify those descending from above. The harmonious interplay of these two, the mento-spiritual and the physico-emotional, is essential to man's well-being.

Health, therefore, is almost entirely a matter of ethics. Health depends upon the mental, the emotional and the physical conduct of life. Psychiatry and psychosomatics as branches of medical science and as therapeutic aids are now demonstrating this fact.

The God Within and the Man Without

Let us look more closely at this idea of a relationship between the Inner Self and the outer self of man. The Inner, Spiritual Self of man continually transmits spiritualising impulses. The mind receives and relays them. The man in his physical body responds to and, in varying degrees, manifests and ratifies them. The extent of such ratification decides the measure of the resultant happiness and health. Similarly, the degree to which they are ignored or violated determines the amount of unhappiness and ill-health experienced in consequence. Where the harmonies are preserved, health is assured. Where they are not preserved, ill-health is inevitable. Long continuing discord within will, in time, produce disease without.

This must be so, for man is not a mere body alone. Man is a threefold being of Spirit, intelligence and body. Moreover, this human power-unit grows increasingly sensitive as evolution proceeds. The nervous and psychic balance and responsiveness of civilised humanity grow continually more delicate. In consequence, violation of basic law produces a greater disturbance in advanced than in primitive man, brings a more keenly felt pain to modern man than to earlier Races.

The Life in all Beings is One Life

What is the message which the Spiritual Self of man transmits, the mind receives and the body must ratify? If it were possible—as it is—to ascend to a state of spiritual consciousness and view the Universe with the eyes of the Spirit, what would be seen? If with the ears of the Spirit the Song of Life could be heard, what would be its theme? The answer, in a phrase, is " Life is One ". There exists but One Life, One Light, One Power, One Love, and that is the central, spiritual truth, in realisation of which the Inner Self of man perpetually abides.

Unity, therefore, is the message which the Higher Self continually transmits to the brain through the medium of the mind. In the savage, the message is scarcely heard and only ratified as an instinct of tribal and family unity. In the self-centredness of material-minded man, unity and love are in many ways denied. " Each for himself and the Devil take the hindmost " is his guiding principle in certain aspects of his life. Individuals, groups, and even Nations, when not threatened by a common danger, still show themselves capable of acting as self-centred units, with little or no regard for the welfare of their fellow men, not to mention the animal kingdom of Nature. The result is clear to every eye. The majority of human beings are prone to ill-health. The chaos, the wars and the threats of wars, the ruin and the disease in the world, are the direct result of man's denial of the truth that Life is one.

Humaneness the Key to Health and Happiness

Is the situation hopeless, then? Is there no cure for war-frightened, disease-ridden humanity? There is hope and there is a cure. Man is gradually evolving. For an increasing number of people the Inner Voice grows stronger, more insistent, calling: " ONE LIFE IN ALL ". Eventually, mind answers and brain and body fulfil. Kindness to fellow men and humaneness to animals then increase. Charity is extended. Love grows deeper, less selfish, more universal. Health and happiness also increase. Ultimately the message of the unity of Life is recognised as a Divine instruction, an impelling summons, an irresistible command. Mind then assents. Brain fully responds. Conduct squares with conscience. Humaneness becomes the gospel of Life. Charity burns as a flame in the heart. Self-interest is lost in selflessness and then, at last, the secret of perfect health, of radiant vitality and of inward happiness has been discovered. *In very truth, recognition and ratification in conduct of the oneness of all Life is the racial and the individual panacea.*

The Case Man has to Answer

What is found when recognition of unity is applied as a test of the mode of life of modern man? Unfortunately, continual disobedience and denial are discovered. What forms do this disobedience and denial more commonly assume? The answer is all too plain. In a word, it is cruelty. Marked characteristics of modern man are cruelty to man and cruelty to beast. The former—cruelty to man—is beyond question. Man's inhumanity to man is proverbial. The Nazi and other Concentration and Labour Camps, the prisons of the world and the Annual Reports of Societies for the Protection of Women and Children, provide convincing proof. Furthermore, man's exploitation and murder of animals is long-continued and world-wide, as Annual Reports of Animal Protection Societies also demonstrate. Man is by far the greatest enemy which the animal kingdom has to fear. For pleasure in blood sports, for food, for adornment, for health, as he thinks, man deliberately and systematically practises the torture and the slaughter of animals.

The laws of harmony and balance are thus repeatedly broken by modern man. The fact of unity is continually denied. The awful retaliation of the law of cause and effect is, in consequence, provoked. Widespread disease, rampant, unpreventable disease, is the result. Those who continually gratify the lust to torture and to kill cannot possibly be either happy or healthy human beings. They are in conflict with the spiritual fact of unity and with the power, the purpose and the spiritual impulse within all Nature. *The wards* [1] *of the physical*

[1] Indentations, etc., in lock and key, designed to prevent other keys from working the lock.

key to health and happiness are now discovered. They are humaneness, kindliness to all living things, benevolence and compassion towards all sentient beings. Simply put, these imply harmony in action.

Four Reasons for Humaneness

Since the virtue of humaneness is of such supreme importance to the health and happiness of man, it merits close examination. Let us look at it together. There are at least four basic reasons for humaneness. The first is that by kindness alone can man ratify the fact of the unity of Life. The One Life has been described as a conscious, hypersensitive, electric, creative energy. All effects, pleasurable or painful, produced upon one living creature are communicated by this electric Life-Force, *elan vital*, throughout the whole of manifested being. Cruelty to sentient Life in one form is cruelty to all, for Life is one. Injury even to a single being can have far-reaching effects, harm to one causing harm to all.

The second reason for humaneness is that universal love is the highest possible ratification in conduct of the fact of unity. One must be humane for love's sake. All else is hate, darkness, disobedience, cosmic lawlessness.

The third reason for humaneness is that the health and the happiness of all sentient beings depend upon their mutual, humane relationship. We are all dependent upon one another for our well-being, progress, fulfilment. Especially are all animals dependent upon man, being helpless before him.

The fourth reason for humaneness is that under the law of compensation, or cause and effect, man reaps as he sows. Cruelty inevitably brings suffering. Kindness most surely brings happiness. Thus humaneness is necessary because Life is one, for love's sake, for happiness' sake and because we reap as we sow.

There can be no evasion, no permanent, scientific self-protection from the results of the breaking of the laws of unity, harmony and love. There are no law-raid shelters. The whole vast product of the modern world's pharmacopoeia and medical practice cannot avail to protect mankind from the results of breaking the law of Life, the very law of being, which is LOVE.

The Crusade for Kindliness

The prevalent ill-health of modern man demonstrates this principle of immutable and inevadable law conclusively. Fortunately, the Crusade for Kindness is growing in volume and power. It is a glorious crusade, for it has two objectives: to banish cruelty from the world and to lead mankind along the way of health and happiness. I repeat that, in addition to the wise conduct of life, humaneness which is obedience to the law of love in thought, feeling, word and deed, is the only way to enduring physical health, as also to lasting world peace.

CHAPTER III

THE THEORY AND PRACTICE OF SPIRITUAL HEALING

Must the Layman always Give Place to the Professional Physician?

CAN bodily changes be produced by the power of the mind and the Spirit? Are all diseases susceptible of cure by spiritual healing alone? What is the rationale of mental and spiritual healing? How may the sufferer co-operate? Is there a simple technique which could be successfully practised by those who do not possess supernormal powers?

Soul and Body

In this broadcast on the important subject of spiritual healing I shall be dealing with one of the highest and most universal of human aspirations—to be able to heal by the powers of mind and of Spirit. The rationale and the method of spiritual healing are worthy of careful consideration, and those listeners who might expect me to go straight to the heart of the matter and provide a method and a formula which can be applied immediately with assurance of success are asked to excuse a somewhat detailed approach to a profound subject. Indeed, I do not believe that a universal panacea exists which can give immediate results.

From the first, it is important to remember that there are physical causes and physical cures of disease. Those who are seriously ill are therefore advised to consult a reputable, reliable physician. At the same time it has now been scientifically demonstrated that the root causes of many of the sufferings of mankind lie deeper than the physical body, having their origin in man's emotional and mental natures. The emergence and rapid development of what has come to be called psychosomatic medicine establish this fact, and point directly to the value of psychological, mental and spiritual methods of healing.

Mind, Emotion and Physical Health

What, then, is psychosomatic medicine? It is based on the fact that the mind and the body are inseparable and together constitute the human being. The word "psychosomatic" is derived from the Greek *psyche*, meaning mind or Soul, and *soma*, the body. It is, therefore, a fresh (in modern days) approach to all medicine. This new attitude recognises the fact that the human being is complex and mysterious, a creature whose brain, emotions and tissues are constantly reacting one upon another. We do some things deliberately. We run or work or eat by our own will, for example. We do not decide to blush with embarrassment or double our heartbeat with rage;

for these actions are controlled by the involuntary or automatic nervous system. Such deep feelings as hate, fear and the need for love, of which we may be wholly or partly unconscious, may find expression through this involuntary system.

If, for instance, a mother is worried over her children's health or is afraid they are not getting along well in school, she may have an attack of indigestion; she has an upset stomach because she is depressed and anxious. If she continues to make herself sick over a sufficient period of time, real damage to the tissues may ensue. A person with a possibly serious gastro-intestinal complaint may go to a doctor. He may find that the illness is caused by emotional tension whereupon, if versed in psychosomatic medicine, he would not only treat the physical ailment but would also look for the cause in the patient's mental or emotional structure, and in his relationship with his environment.

Psychosomatic Medicine

Dr. John A. Schindler, Chief Physician of the Munroe Clinic, broadcasting over the University of Wisconsin Radio Station, said that psychosomatic illness is not produced by a bacterium, by virus or by a new growth. It is produced by the circumstances of daily living and the chief causes are cares, difficulties, troubles.

Theosophy agrees, teaching that we do not think with the brain alone. Thinking involves the entire body in a series of complicated nerve impulses that centre in the brain. Anger, for example, causes the face to become white or red, the eyes to widen, the muscles to tighten and cause trembling. Embarrassment produces dilation of the blood vessels in the face and this causes blushing. Emotion affects the endocrine system. Sudden acute fear, such as a near motor smash, sends an impulse to the adrenal glands which squeeze adrenalin into the system, thereby causing palpitation of the heart.

This consideration of the physical effect of thoughts and feelings leads us directly to our subject of spiritual healing. How may this be achieved? What are the parts played respectively by healer and sufferer? How may they best co-operate? The answers to these questions—as, in fact, to every other question concerning humanity—are dependent upon knowledge of the true nature of man.

What is Man?

What, then, is man? Theosophy answers that he is primarily a thinker, hence his name; for the word " man " comes from the Sanskrit *man*, meaning " to think ". He is also, however, a being of emotion and of physical activity, whilst overshadowing and acting through thought, emotion, word and deed is the Innermost Self of man, his Immortal Soul, the Divine Spirit in him. This brings us to a profound truth, which is that the Spiritual Soul of man is for ever at one with the Source of its existence. Man-Spirit and God-Spirit are one Spirit. When this begins to be realised, when the Divine Power and Presence within man begins to be known, then that mighty Power can be tapped and released for the service of one's fellow men.

The Inner Self and the Divine Life

The first step in preparing oneself to become a spiritual healer, therefore, is self-discovery. The Innermost Self, the Divine Presence, should be sought by means of regular, daily meditation. Thereafter, by the regular practice of spiritual healing, the faculty may be developed of drawing upon the Power within, transmuting it for the help of those in need.

We are thus presented with the concept of man as a power unit through whom the Divine, Creative Life-force flows continually. Man, in his spiritual nature, may be regarded as relaying throughout his whole being Power from the inexhaustible, universal Source, which is God. The unimpeded, rhythmic flow of this energy throughout man's nature is essential to health and happiness, for the Creative Life of God is a mighty and irresistible force. When it flows freely through a man it vitalises him, and can heal him when he is sick. Resistance to this force in thought, feeling and action, sets up friction, discordance and distortion, which can cause physical malfunction and disease.

What is Health?

We are now able to give a definition of health. In terms of dynamics, health is the unimpeded, rhythmic flow of Power, Life and Consciousness from the Inner, Higher Self of man through all his vehicles. Ill-health comes to us because somewhere in our nature a condition exists which obstructs, diverts from its proper channels, or imparts a discordance to, the universal Life-force. Spiritual healing can remove these interior obstructions, these barriers at the mental, the emotional and the physical levels.

Obstructions

How are these barriers set up within us? By our violation of the law of love and the principle of the unity of Life. This violation takes two forms, the objective and the subjective. Objectively, selfishness and cruelty in word and deed set up discordances within us. Hurting others is one of the root causes of suffering, not only for those who are hurt but, under the law of cause and effect, for the very people who violate the principle of unity by needlessly inflicting pain. Such, then, is one objective cause of barriers to the free flow throughout man's nature of God's creative Life-force. These barriers must be swept away before health can be fully restored. Mental and spiritual healing with the full co-operation of the sufferer—particularly in self-correction—are the most effective means of accomplishing this.

Subjectively, barriers are set up and ill-health is generated by our thoughts and feelings of hate, dislike, desire to dominate, bitterness, anger, malice and unforgivingness. These are veritable toxins and they can poison the bodily system. A simple but sure recipe for good health and happiness is to cease from hurting others. As I have said, however, there is another way in which we bring ill-health upon ourselves; it is by the misuse of our bodies, for the body is indeed a temple [1] of the God-Self within and the potential vehicle by means of which the Inner Soul, the true Self, gains the experience necessary to its evolutionary progress. Thus we see that health depends upon ethics and upon right conduct in thought, word, deed, diet and habits of life.

The healer's true purpose, then, is to help the sufferer to re-orient the mind, and more especially to adopt a right attitude towards life. His task is to remove interior barriers and restore the harmonious flow of the inner Life throughout the whole nature of the sufferer. Successfully applied, spiritual healing brings down an immense flood of Divine Life which can revitalise and heal mind, emotion and body.

A Formula for Health

How may the suppliant co-operate? First and foremost by a genuine and sincere endeavour to correct errors in character, thought, feeling and the conduct of life. The mental attitude of the patient should be one of intelligent acceptance of misfortune, based upon recognition of personal responsibility under the law of cause and effect. Above all, there must be neither resentment nor bitterness.

[1] I *Cor.* III. 16.

Here are five rules which those who seek spiritual healing—indeed all who would achieve and maintain health and happiness—would do well to obey:—

1. Cultivate a state of goodwill to all people, never by thought, word or deed unnecessarily hurting any other person. Harmoniousness and harmlessness to all are the great preventives against ill-health.
2. Develop a habit of happiness. The perfect lubricant for stiff joints is the oil of joy.
3. Do not nurse grievances. Deliberately forgive all who have hurt you, as you hope to be forgiven by those whom you may have hurt.
4. Send out affection to all. As harmlessness prevents, so loving kindness cures disease and suffering.
5. Link up regularly every day with the one great Source of spiritual power and blessing which is within you, for by this means the outer, personal nature becomes empowered and unified and a true, dedicated attitude towards life is developed and maintained.

Such are five rules for health and happiness. Both healers and suppliants should obey them.

The statement that such actions can actually cure disease may sound far-fetched. In reality they do far more than cure disease—they prevent it. Goodwill, the habit of happiness, forgiveness and loving kindness, combined with an intelligent way of living, produce good health, just as their opposites produce ill-health.

A Healing Ritual

Now for the actual process of spiritual healing, whether the sufferers are present or not. Here is a simple but highly effective method, which may be used either when one is alone or working with a group.

First, have a list of the Christian and surnames of those to be healed. Then, in complete privacy and with the body relaxed, turn the thoughts in powerful concentration to a recognised Healing Source. For most Christians, doubtless, this will be the Lord Christ, the Great Healer of Men. Visualise Him and reverently draw near to Him, seeking to realise His Presence. With half-minute pauses for concentration and visualisation after each phrase, repeat aloud and with powerful intent the following Invocation:

> " May the healing power of the Lord Christ descend upon......................

Here mention the Christian and the surnames of those to be healed, with a five-second pause between each name. During the pause visualise the sufferers as radiantly well and as in the very Presence of the Lord Christ, flooded by His glorious healing power and golden light. After all the names have been mentioned, continue:

> " May Christ's healing power descend upon them all and may the Holy Angels encompass them."

After a further pause say:

> " May the light of Christ's love enfold them forever. Amen."

Those who will sincerely, selflessly and regularly follow this procedure will indubitably prove to themselves that any reasonably intelligent, unselfish person can heal effectively by the powers of the mind and the Spirit.

PART SEVEN

ANIMAL WELFARE: MAN'S GREAT RESPONSIBILITY

CHAPTER I

THE GOSPEL OF HUMANENESS

The Need for Humaneness

WHY is it necessary to organise World Week for Animal Welfare? Because of two opposite influences apparent in the world today. What are these? One is a growing humaneness towards animals and the other is a growing cruelty. An example of man's growing humaneness is the action of Mr. H. G. Wells, who in 1940 published in the London *Times* his " Rights of Man ". It consists of eleven Clauses, Clause 11 reading as follows:—

> " That a Charter of Rights for the animal kingdom be drawn up by international consultation, and that all individuals enjoying the benefits of security and freedom conferred by [the other Clauses of] this human Charter [of the Rights of Man] resolve that they will uphold and observe the provisions of the Charter for the animals who are not able to speak for themselves, but who look to man nevertheless for protection against undue slaughter, starvation, neglect, cruelty or exploitation."

The Prevalence of Cruelty

This was a courageous act, for Mr. Wells threw himself open to the scorn of so-called *practical* men and ran the risk of weakening his standing as a thinker, a leader, a statesman and a scientist. Mankind as a whole is very far from ready for a Charter granting to members of the animal kingdom equal rights with man of citizenship of the earth. Nevertheless, despite the attitude of the majority, during the last hundred years the Cause of Animal Welfare has attracted and influenced increasing numbers of people. The ideal of granting to animals rights of citizenship equal to those now possessed by man is not, therefore, really hopeless of fulfilment.

Every year since 1928, during World Week for Animals—the first week in October of each year—the Cause of Humaneness is made the subject of public thought and demonstration throughout the free world. In addition, numerous Movements have arisen to protect animals from their greatest enemy—man. Amongst these Movements are:

(1) Societies for the Prevention of Cruelty to Animals.
(2) Societies for the Abolition of Vivisection.
(3) Campaigns for the Humane Killing of food animals—recently successful in New Zealand.
(4) The International Vegetarian Union.
(5) The American Vegetarian Union.
(6) The various Vegetarian Societies throughout the world.
(7) The Universities Federation for Animal Welfare (U.F.A.W.), Britain.
(8) Mr. Wells' Charter, " The Rights of Man ".

The Crusade for Kindness

Thus the great gospel of humaneness continues to find its supporters and its crusaders. They are still but a small minority, however, and an immense work remains to be done. A veritable army of opponents of cruelty, of workers for humaneness, is needed to advance the great Cause. Mr. Wells' Charter is a great encouragement, especially to those who believe in a law of cause and effect. It is, I suggest, a sign of an awakening spiritual consciousness in man, a deepening sense of kinship with all living beings and a recognition of the oneness of all Life.

During World Week for Animal Welfare a great call for humaneness is sent out. We are all reminded that every active crusader for kindness and gentleness to animals diminishes the power of evil in the world. Every practising humanitarian reduces the amount of suffering and cruelty on all sides. The Animal Clause in Mr. Wells' Charter must be fully implemented. Every form of cruelty to animals must be attacked and stopped.

Education must one day take up this Cause. Children must be instructed concerning the proper place of animals on earth and their true relationship to man. Their rightful place is that of members of a sentient kingdom of Nature at present occupying a subhuman rung of the evolutionary ladder which all Life is ascending. Their true relationship to man is that of younger brothers to be protected by him and to be lifted by every means within his power to the next phase of their evolution, which is entry into the human kingdom of Nature. The growing humaneness of modern man will surely be the force which will bring about these needed reforms.

The Case Man has to Answer

Unfortunately, and somewhat paradoxically as it would seem, doubtless owing partly to the increase of the population on the planet, this advance is accompanied by an increase and an accentuation of the cruelty upon the earth. Indeed, the citadel of cruelty to animals has now become so firmly founded, so scientifically planned and established, that our position as crusaders for kindness to animals might appear to be almost as hopeless as was that of Britain at the time of the withdrawal from Dunkirk. Thus, despite the growing humaneness in the world, the preponderance over the humanitarians of the inflictors of unneccesary suffering upon animals appears to be increasing. Hence the necessity for World Week for Animals. Here are the charges we have to answer:

(1) We kill animals, often in the cruellest manner, for religious sacrifices.

(2) We kill elephants for their tusks.

(3) We kill whales for their oil and their flesh, firing bombs into their sensitive bodies.

(4) We kill innumerable birds for their flesh and their feathers.

(5) We kill most cruelly hordes of animals for their flesh and their hides.

(6) We kill horses, sometimes when in foal, for their flesh.

(7) We hunt, wound and kill animals for the sake of "sport".

(8) We boil countless millions of shellfish alive annually.

(9) We torture and kill millions of animals in vivisection experiments.

(10) We kill and torture bulls in bull fights to make a public spectacle.

(11) Our existence is based upon bloodshed and agony.

(12) We adorn ourselves with cruelty—fur for coats, feathers for our hats.

(13) Our homes are thus saturated with cruelty, and we in them.

(14) We make of sacred Christmas a butchery of creatures and thus deny the universal love and tenderness which the Christ was born to bring to all mankind.

(15) When peace came, the animal kingdom had nothing to look forward to except increased savagery, persecution and torture of the most horrible kind which the ingenuity of man enables him to devise.

In case I should appear to be exaggerating, or at best over-stressing the amount of cruelty inflicted upon animals by man, here is a recent estimate of the number of animals, birds and fishes slaughtered annually for human consumption, or otherwise unnecessarily exploited, injured, tortured and killed.

Animals, Etc.	Number Killed or Injured Annually	Method of Killing
CATTLE—Calves, Oxen, Cows, Heifers, Horses, Ponies, Foals.	200,000,000	Mostly pole-axed. Probably less than 5% killed by humane slaughter.
SHEEP—Lambs, Rams, Ewes.	400,000,000	Mostly pole-axed as above.

Animals, Etc.	Number Killed or Injured Annually	Method of Killing
PIGS—Sows, Boars, etc.	200,000,000	Throats cut, or by mechanical killers.
RABBITS	1,000,000,000	Trapped or shot; some gassed.
BIRDS—Poultry, Hens and Cocks, Chickens, Geese, Ducks, Pheasants, Swans, Turkeys, etc.	2,000,000,000	Necks twisted.
SMALLER BIRDS	1,000,000,000	Shooting and netting.
FISHES AND REPTILES	10,000,000,000	Mostly by nets, and left to die.
VIVISECTION	20,000,000	Probably less than a million with any anaesthetic.
FURS AND SKINS	200,000,000	Trapped in most cases and left to die.
HUNTING—Lions, Tigers, Foxes, Deer, Otters, etc.	1,000,000	Shooting and trapping.
Total ..	15,021,000,000	

Such, in part, is the case man has to answer. Such is the call of "World Week for Animals". Such is our work as builders of a New World Order. May the day of harmlessness, of gentleness and of love soon dawn upon our earth.

CHAPTER II

THE HUMANE SLAUGHTER OF FOOD ANIMALS

This Interview, with minor, local variations, was transmitted from Commercial Stations in Melbourne, Hobart and Brisbane.

Announcer: Why is the humane killing of food animals by a mechanical instrument so important?

Mr. Hodson: Because it does away with the throat-cutting and the neck-breaking of fully-conscious animals.

A. How is humane slaughtering done?

H. Either by a rifle, or by a captive bolt pistol which renders the animal instantly unconscious.

A. What are the main arguments in favour of humane killing? Why is it favoured?

H. Here are some of the reasons: In the slaughter of animals for food, the use of the hammer to stun cattle and the throat-cutting and neck-breaking of fully-conscious animals are obsolete and are the cause of much needless suffering. All too often, to become skilled in these methods the learner must practise on fully-conscious animals, with appalling results in many cases.

An alternative and humane way of slaughtering, certain in action, is possible—namely, by the use of the Humane Killer. This method is used in England and Scotland, on the Continent of Europe and in New Zealand. In many countries humane killing is compulsory.

A. Is this method of slaughtering by a humane killing instrument quite efficient?

H. Completely so. Tests by the Royal Society for the Prevention of Cruelty to Animals in England have demonstrated both the complete efficiency and the humaneness of stunning and killing by this method.

A. Is the appliance costly?

H. No. The approximate capital cost of the Humane Killer in Australian currency is either £15 or £8, according to the type used. Cartridges of the captive bolt type, which is most in use, cost approximately one penny per beast.

A. That is not at all expensive.

H. No, it isn't. It is considered by competent authority, moreover, that owing to the greater speed and effectiveness of humane killing instruments, the actual cost of slaughtering can be reduced below the present price.

A. What about the meat of animals so killed? Does it keep quite well?

H. The quality of the meat humanely slaughtered is not adversely affected in any respect whatsoever.

A. What do users of the Humane Killer Pistol report?

H. Scotland secured an Act of Parliament in 1928 requiring that animals be instantaneously slaughtered or stunned by a mechanically operated instrument in proper repair. This Act is still in force.

The Medical Officer of Health for Southampton, Dr. Lauder, wrote after four years: "The by-law in force in this Borough for Humane Slaughtering of Animals has been in operation for the past four years with satisfactory results. With the mechanical instruments now in use, suffering has been reduced to a minimum, with no detrimental effect to the meat."

The British Board of Agriculture strongly advised that such instruments be used, adopted them on all cattle-carrying boats, and imposed their use upon all butchers in their employment. The use of the Captive Bolt Gun on all sheep slaughtered was ordered by the English Board of Agriculture soon after the commencement of the last war.

The British Admiralty long ago adopted the appliances in all its own departments, where they have ever since been in use with unvarying success.

A. What about the Continent of Europe? Is the Pistol used there?

H. In some countries it is. In 1893 the Government of Switzerland passed an Act forbidding butchers to kill without previous stunning. Germany, Denmark, Italy, Holland and Scandinavia, and now New Zealand, have followed this example. The use of the Captive Bolt Pistol complies with the requirements of the Mohammedan Religion. It is evident, there fore, that the case for humane slaughter is unanswerable.

A. Are the ordinary methods of slaughter really very cruel?

H. No one who has stood at the killing pens and watched the stunning and slaughtering of food animals will deny that there is much needless suffering involved in the present methods. To be killed by having a bullet fired into the brain, causing instantaneous unconsciousness, is one thing. To die slowly by being hung upside down by one hind leg, and having a knife driven into one's throat whilst fully conscious, as some cattle are, and then left to bleed to death, is quite another.

No financial loss is involved where reasonable precautions are taken and the work properly organised, for blood splash is not evident where animals are rested before killing and bled promptly. In consequence, as I have said, the keeping qualities of meat killed by the Humane Killer, whether for immediate consumption or for export to hot climates, are at least equal to those of meat killed by older methods.

A. Is there a book one can read telling about all this?

H. Yes, there are several. The Royal Society for the Prevention of Cruelty to Animals (Incorporated), England, put the whole matter to the test. The Society then issued a booklet entitled *Humane Slaughtering: The Verdict of Experience and Scientific Tests.* Details of the various tests are therein recorded, also one hundred and twenty statements from Meat Traders in all departments of butchery and from officials of Local Authorities in England, including butchers, Meat Inspectors, Abattoir Superintendents, Town Clerks, Medical Officers of Health, Sanitary Inspectors, Veterinary Officers and a Professor of Veterinary Science. All these testify from regular experience of the use of Humane Killers that "they save a vast amount of needless suffering and that their use is not detrimental to the meat or other products of the animal." Their evidence is couched in decisive and forthright language which should satisfy even the most critical.

A. What, in general terms, is the reform you are proposing?

H. That all sheep, cattle and swine slaughtered in abattoirs or slaughter-houses should be instantaneously rendered unconscious by shooting or the use of the Captive Bolt Gun, or—as an alternative in the case of pigs, for example—by stunning with electricity. There is no ground whatever for delay, and legislation should be enacted to make humane killing by mechanical instruments compulsory throughout Australia.

* * * * *

Since this broadcast was delivered, legislation has been enacted in Victoria making compulsory the use of the Captive Bolt Pistol for the slaughter of food animals.

A SUMMING UP: SOME CENTRAL THEOSOPHICAL IDEAS[1]

A Fundamental Truth

THE term "Theosophia" was coined by an old Greek Philosopher from two Greek words—*Theo* and *Sophia*. It means, literally, Divine Wisdom or actually, all-Truth. The more modern form of the word "Theosophy" means the same, namely: the totality of truth allotted to man on this planet. Theosophy has also been defined as a spiritual philosophy of life consistent with science.

A central idea is that of the inseparable unity of the Spirit of each man with the Universal Spirit, or God. Man-Spirit and God-Spirit are one Spirit. Furthermore, says Theosophy, this fact can become known by man. Regular prayer and wisely directed meditation can bring the human mind into such close attunement with the Divine Spirit of the Universe, that the exaltation of union and communion with God may be experienced. Theosophy also teaches clearly and in detail how this conscious unity with God may be achieved.

One part of the intellectual appeal of Theosophy consists of its logical answers to the problems of human

[1] This Talk was transmitted through all Australian National Stations, and not from Station 2GB.

life. Take, for example, justice for man on earth. The existence of undeserved human suffering, especially of newly-born children, seems to be a denial of justice. Dryden posed this question by saying: " Virtue in distress and vice in triumph make atheists of mankind." Is human life, especially when it first begins at birth, based upon chance or luck—good, bad or indifferent—or is there law, justice, logic, in human experience? Theosophy answers unhesitatingly and positively; law, justice, logic. How, then, does it explain apparent injustice, as, for example, when a baby is born blind, deaf, dumb, diseased, malformed, mentally deficient? How can there be justice, fair play, in that? Theosophy answers: the Soul of such a child has been born on earth before, has committed sins in a former life and is reaping in the new life as it has sown in a preceding one, under the unbreakable law of cause and effect.

St. Paul was thus proclaiming pure Theosophy when he said: " God is not mocked: for whatsoever a man soweth that shall he also reap." [1] Our Lord also said: " Till heaven and earth pass, one jot or one tittle shall in no wise pass from the law, till all be fulfilled." [2]

Evolution through Successive Lives on Earth

If, however, there is only one life on earth, these statements cannot be true. But if man incarnates many times during his evolution to perfection and cause and effect operate from life to life, then

[1] *Gal.* VI. 1.

[2] *Matt.* V. 18.

affirmations of causative law are true and human life is founded upon law, justice, logic. Think of the alternative. Without reincarnation and cause and effect, life is a hopeless riddle which defies solution. With reincarnation and cause and effect, the problem of apparent injustice is solved, for very often we sow in one life and reap in the next. Our present conditions, therefore, are the product of our own past actions. Our future, then, is in our own hands; we can make of it what we will. Such are three only of the many inspiring and mentally satisfying teachings of Theosophy.

Let me repeat them as I close. Firstly, the Spirit of man and the Spirit which is God are one Spirit. By prayer, man can know this unity with God. Secondly, man lives many lives on earth on his way to perfection, and thirdly, the law of cause and effect, or sowing and reaping, ensures perfect justice to every man.

LIST OF BOOKS FOR BEGINNERS IN THEOSOPHY, IN THE ORDER IN WHICH THEY MAY BE READ

For Study

An Outline of Theosophy	... C. W. Leadbeater.
A Textbook of Theosophy	... ,,
First Principles of Theosophy, and other works	... C. Jinarajadasa.
The Ancient Wisdom	... A. Besant.
The Great Plan	... ,,
Man, Visible and Invisible	... C. W. Leadbeater.
Thought Forms	... A. Besant and C. W. Leadbeater.
Thought Power, Its Control and Culture	... A. Besant.
An Introduction to Yoga	... ,,
The Manuals of Theosophy, Nos. 1 to 7	... A. Besant and C. W. Leadbeater.
Invisible Helpers	... C. W. Leadbeater.
Esoteric Christianity	... A. Besant.
The Christian Creed	... C. W. Leadbeater.
The Inner Life, Vols. I and II	,,

The Hidden Side of Things, Vols. I and II ... C. W. Leadbeater.
The Masters ... A. Besant.
The Inner Government of the World ... ,,
In the Outer Court ... ,,
The Path of Discipleship ... ,,
Initiation, the Perfecting of Man ... ,,
The Masters and The Path ... C. W. Leadbeater.
The Light of Asia ... Sir Edwin Arnold.
The Song Celestial ... ,,
Mount Everest ... G. S. Arundale.
A Theosophist Looks at the World ... N. Sri Ram.
The Human Interest ... ,,
An Approach to Reality ... ,,
Man: His Origins and Evolution ... ,,
Destiny ... Geoffrey Hodson.
The Brotherhood of Angels and of Men ... ,, ,,
The Angelic Hosts ... ,, ,,
Reincarnation: Fact or Fallacy? ,, ,,
The Seven Human Temperaments ... ,, ,,
The Miracle of Birth ... ,, ,,
The Kingdom of the Gods ... ,, ,,
Old Diary Leaves, Vols. I, II, III ... H. S. Olcott.

15

Reference Books:

The Etheric Double ...	A. E. Powell	Indexed compilations which all serious students should possess.
The Astral Body ...	,,	
The Mental Body ...	,,	
The Causal Body ...	,,	
The Solar System ...	,,	
The Key to Theosophy ...	H. P. Blavatsky.	
Isis Unveiled ...	,,	
The Secret Doctrine ...	,,	
The Theosophical Glossary ...	,,	
Letters from the Masters of the Wisdom (Compilations) ...	C. Jinarajadasa.	
The Mahatma Letters to A. P. Sinnett (Transcribed and Compiled) ...	A. T. Barker.	
The Science of the Sacraments...	C. W. Leadbeater.	
The Hidden Side of Christian Festivals ...	,,	
The Chakras ...	,,	
Talks on the Path of Occultism	A. Besant and C. W. Leadbeater.	
The Lives of Alcyone ...	,, ,,	
Man: Whence, How and Whither? ...	,, ,,	
The Story of Atlantis	Scott Elliott.	
Kundalini ...	G. S. Arundale.	
The Lotus Fire ...	,,	
The Science of Seership ...	Geoffrey Hodson.	
Some Experiments in Four-Dimensional Vision ...	,, ,,	

Devotional Books:

Christ and Buddha, and all the smaller books ...	C. Jinarajadasa.
The K. H. Letters to C. W. Leadbeater and other Compilations ...	,,
The Practice of the Presence of God ...	Brother Lawrence.
Spiritual Maxims ...	,, ,,
At the Feet of the Master ...	J. Krishnamurti.
The Doctrine of the Heart ...	A. Besant.
The Bhagavad Gita (Translated)	,,
Viveka Chudamani (Translated)	M. Chatterji.
Light on the Path ...	M. Collins.
The Idyll of the White Lotus...	,,
The Voice of the Silence ...	H. P. Blavatsky.
The Gospel of the Buddha ...	Paul Carus.
The Life of the Lord Buddha ...	L. Adams Beck.
Thoughts for Aspirants ...	N. Sri Ram.
Meditations on the Occult Life...	Geoffrey Hodson.
Be Ye Perfect ...	,, ,,
Thus Have I Heard ...	,, ,,

Occult Fiction:

John Silence ...	Algernon Blackwood.
The Education of Uncle Paul...	,, ,,
The Bright Messenger ...	,, ,,
The Centaur, and other works...	,, ,,
A Brother of the Shadow ...	Grace Colmore.
The Ninth Vibration ...	L. Adams Beck.

The Treasure of Ho	... L. Adams Beck.
The Garden of Vision	... ,,
The House of Fulfilment	... ,,
The Splendour of Asia, and other works	... ,,
Om	... Talbot Mundy.
Zanoni	... B. Lytton.
The Coming Race	... ,,
Peter Ibbotson	... Du Maurier.
The Perfume of Egypt	... C. W. Leadbeater.
The Caves and Jungles of Hindustan	... H. P. Blavatsky.
Karma	... A. P. Sinnett.
The Youngest Disciple	... Edward Thompson.